Partner Poems & Word Ladders

for Building Foundational Literacy Skills

DAVID L. HARRISON, TIMOTHY V. RASINSKI, AND MARY JO FRESCH

Editor: Maria L. Chang
Cover design: Tannaz Fassihi
Cover and interior art: Julissa Mora
Interior design: Maria Lilja

ISBN: 978-1-338-79290-4
Scholastic Inc., 557 Broadway, New York, NY 10012.
Copyright © 2022 by David L. Harrison, Timothy V. Rasinski, and Mary Jo Fresch.
Published by Scholastic Inc. All rights reserved.
Printed in the U.S.A.
First printing, January 2022.

1 2 3 4 5 6 7 8 9 10   40   30 29 28 27 26 25 24 23 22

Table of Contents

Meet the Authors

Hello.

I'm David, the poet. My job is to write poems that you can use with your kids. Why verse? Because it rhymes (usually) and has meter (almost always), so its structured language makes it a wonderful classroom tool for learning the poem itself and appreciating the cadence and natural beauty of our language.

Research also tells us that reading as partners further encourages and strengthens children's reading skills. That's why our book takes full advantage of structured language's special qualities by focusing on poems for two or more voices. In this book you'll find 26 original poems, each written for partner reading. I hope you and your students enjoy reading and playing with them as much as I loved writing them for you.

I want to say how happy I am to be partnering with Tim and Mary Jo. In 2009, Tim and I published *Partner Poems for Building Fluency* (Scholastic Teaching Resources), and in 2013, Mary Jo and I wrote *Learning Through Poetry* (Shell Education), a set of five books that featured 96 poems, each inspired by a different phoneme. And now, lucky me, I get to do a book with both of them together!

DAVID L. HARRISON, Litt.D.
Poet Laureate
Drury University

Dear Colleagues:

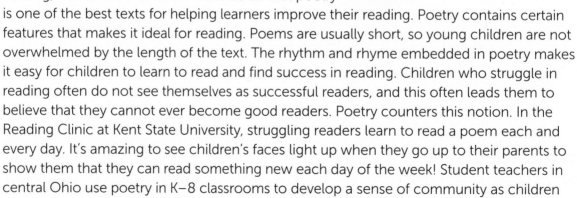

Mary Jo and I are the professor parts of this endeavor. After years of working with young readers and children who experience difficulty in reading, we have come to the conclusion that poetry is one of the best texts for helping learners improve their reading. Poetry contains certain features that makes it ideal for reading. Poems are usually short, so young children are not overwhelmed by the length of the text. The rhythm and rhyme embedded in poetry makes it easy for children to learn to read and find success in reading. Children who struggle in reading often do not see themselves as successful readers, and this often leads them to believe that they cannot ever become good readers. Poetry counters this notion. In the Reading Clinic at Kent State University, struggling readers learn to read a poem each and every day. It's amazing to see children's faces light up when they go up to their parents to show them that they can read something new each day of the week! Student teachers in central Ohio use poetry in K–8 classrooms to develop a sense of community as children

Partner Poems & Word Ladders for Building Foundational Literacy Skills: K–2 © by Harrison, Rasinski & Fresch, Scholastic Teaching Solutions

read and laugh together. These student teachers soon discover the power of rhyme and rhythm. They leave their teaching experience ready to use poetry across the curriculum and throughout the day.

Poetry can contain wonderful words that can easily contribute to children's vocabulary development. Moreover, since words in poems often rhyme, poetry lends itself extremely well to children's phonics development (e.g., *If I can read the word* peep *in "Little Bo Peep," I can learn to read* beep, deep, seep, sleep, sweep, steeple, *and many more*). Poems are meant to be read aloud and performed, so children need to rehearse or read them repeatedly. Repeated reading is one of the best ways to develop reading fluency in children. Poems also contain wonderful and meaningful content that can lead to great discussions that build comprehension. And poems can cross the curriculum. The content of a poem might be just the way to start a science unit on bugs or a social studies unit on mapping.

Reading is also a social activity. To perform a poem, you need an audience. Some poems are written to be recited by more than one reader. We call these "partner poems." David Harrison is one of the very best poets for children around, and he is particularly gifted at writing partner poems.

In light of all this, we happily partnered with David to develop this book for you and your students. Each delightful poem in this collection is meant to be read by two or more readers. Following each poem are Word Ladders, a popular instructional activity that helps children build and learn new words as well as develop their phonics and spelling skills in a fun, gamelike way. Think of all the word games we play as adults. Have you noticed that if you play those games regularly you get better at them? We have a special name for when you get better at something—it's called *learning*! And speaking of learning, each poem also comes with a mini-lesson designed to help children develop proficiency in critical reading, language arts, and curricular competencies.

As you can see, each poem in this book is essentially a complete lesson you can employ with your students, whether you teach a classroom full of children or work as an interventionist with small groups. Children will enjoy reading our poems, playing with words, and developing important reading skills. What could be better than that? Above all, we hope that you and your learners will take great delight in the wonderful poems that David Harrison brings to this book.

We wish you and your students lots of fun, plenty of reading, and much progress in building literacy skills.

TIMOTHY RASINSKI, Ph.D.
Professor of Literacy Education
Kent State University

MARY JO FRESCH, Ph.D.
Professor Emerita and Academy Professor
The Ohio State University

What's in This Book

Using lively partner poems along with engaging Word Ladders and mini-lessons, this comprehensive resource offers a hands-on, ready approach for helping children develop phonics skills, fluency, spelling, word analysis skills, vocabulary, comprehension, and more.

Each partner poem focuses on a particular phonogram, based on the research of Edward Fry (1998) and Wylie and Durrell (1970). Using texts that focus on phonograms provide "early entry into reading for young children" (Menon & Hiebert, 2005, p. 17). In the International Literacy Association's "What's Hot in Literacy" 2020 report, respondents agreed that "building early literacy skills through a balanced approach that combines both foundational and language comprehension instruction" is critical.

How did we decide on which phonograms to use? Edward Fry discovered that by adding beginning consonants, blends, and digraphs to the 38 most common phonograms found in English, 654 words can be made. Wylie and Durrell similarly identified 37 frequently occurring phonograms that appear in more than 500 primary-level words. The research-based lists of Fry and Wylie and Durrell are highly regarded as providing powerful, independent decoding skills to young readers. Both lists share 26 phonograms in common; Fry suggests 12 more, and Wylie and Durrell found 11 others. Combining these lists provides 49 phonograms and offers a unique approach not found in any other publications. In our work with young readers, we have found a few additional phonograms that will expand their ability to work across words: -oat, -oo, and -ow (diphthong).

We divided the phonograms into two books. This book, for Grades K–2, features those phonograms most appropriate for younger learners (boldfaced in the chart below). Its companion book, for Grades 1–3, highlights the other phonograms and provides practice for slightly more experienced readers who are ready to expand their vocabulary and experiences with print.

Of course, the power of these phonograms is not limited to primary-level words. These rimes appear in literally thousands of multisyllabic words; for example, *am = ambulance, camera; ack = acknowledge, backpack; ot = otter, apricot; eed = proceed, seedling.* Providing engaging poems that use these phonograms helps children improve their ability to decode as well as their reading fluency and comprehension.

ab	**ack**	**ag**	ail
ain	ake	ale	**am**
ame	**an**	**ank**	**ap**
ash	**at**	ate	aw
ay	eat	**ed**	eed
ell	est	ew	ice
ick	ide	ight	**ill**
im	**in**	ine	**ing**
ink	**ip**	**it**	oat
ob	ock	oke	**op**
ore	**ot**	out	ow
uck	**ug**	**um**	**ump**
unk	**y**	oo (oon/ook/oom)	ow (diphthong)

How to Use This Book

This book includes 26 partner poems—one for each featured phonogram—written for two or more readers. The phonograms are listed alphabetically, but you can select any poem that might tie into your ongoing word study or language arts lessons. This makes this resource useful throughout the school year, allowing you to use the poems whenever they naturally fit best in your curriculum.

After you've selected a poem, display it on your board for a whole-class read-aloud and make photocopies for children to practice reading with a partner. Give children plenty of opportunities to read each poem aloud several times. This builds fluency and confidence with the vocabulary. We also recommend having each child keep a notebook of the poems so children can revisit them. The poems can be familiar texts to use during independent reading. You may also reuse a poem when you feel the need to review a particular feature or use it with a different activity.

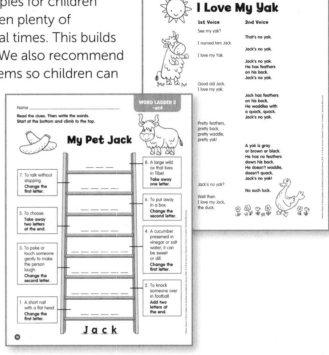

Following each poem are two reproducible Word Ladders that can be used for partner work, in small groups, or with the whole class. Working with Word Ladders is a proven approach for helping children develop their decoding, phonics, spelling, and vocabulary skills in a fun, gamelike way. Word Ladder 1 focuses on phonics and gives children practice on the featured phonogram, while Word Ladder 2 emphasizes vocabulary and may be a bit more challenging.

Word Ladders are easy to implement, and each one takes only about 10 minutes to complete. Simply follow these steps:

1. After children have read, rehearsed, and performed each partner poem, make a copy of the companion Word Ladders for each child. (You may want to start with the simpler Word Ladder 1.)

2. Read aloud the first word at the bottom of the ladder. Invite children to spell the word. Discuss the meaning and any important orthographic (spelling) features of the word.

When a Poem Is "Hard"

Some children, especially those in kindergarten, may find the poems a bit challenging. We feel that children like challenges. Moreover, research has shown that children can accelerate their reading development when given the opportunity to practice and achieve mastery over challenging texts.

When a poem is challenging for children, you need to provide them with more support and scaffolding. You can do so by displaying an enlarged copy of the poem and reading it aloud while pointing to the words and having children follow along silently. Read the poem with the children chorally multiple times. Have children read while listening to a recorded version of the poem or with a classroom volunteer or with a classmate. And, of course, encourage parents to read the poem with their children multiple times at home, helping them toward the goal of reading (and performing) the poem in class as well as at home for family members.

Partner Poems & Word Ladders for Building Foundational Literacy Skills: K–2 © by Harrison, Rasinski & Fresch, Scholastic Teaching Solutions

3. Guide children in working their way up the ladder. For each new word on the ladder, have children read the clues that will help them figure out and spell each new word. Each word comes with three kinds of clues:

   a. the definition of the new word or a sentence in which the word is used in a meaningful context but left out for children to fill in

   b. the kind of spelling changes children need to make to the previous word in order to build the new word (for example, "change one letter," "take away one letter," "add two letters," or "move the letters around")

   c. the number of letter spaces to make the new word

   Be sure to add your own clues and supports as you go through the words with your students. Perhaps a recent event in your classroom can act as a clue. If a word is challenging, you might just want to say the word to children and expand on its meaning. See if they can write the word from a pronunciation of it. Then check and discuss its meaning.

4. The final word in each Word Ladder is often related to the first word as well as to the poem children have just read. Children love being challenged to figure out what that last word will be on their own.

A language arts mini-lesson in reading, writing, or word study also accompanies each poem. A short list of related words containing the phonogram comes with each lesson so you can extend the word study and connect the poem to other content studies. Words used in the poem are boldfaced. The lists are organized by single consonant onsets, consonant blends, and more complex words. In addition, "Wondering About..." examines words used in the poem that "sound" like the phonogram, but are spelled differently. This gives you an opportunity to dive into word histories or puzzle out with children why some words sound similar but have different spellings.

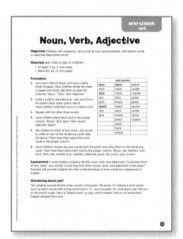

Not Intended for Independent Work

We cannot emphasize enough that the poems, Word Ladders, and mini-lessons in this book are intended for you, the teacher, to help children become fluent readers and wordsmiths. Children learn best when you guide them as they build fluency with the poems, master the words in the Word Ladders, and achieve success in the mini-lessons. Some of the words in these activities may not be familiar to children. This is your chance to teach them. When children experience difficulty with a poem, Word Ladder, or mini-lesson, use this opportunity to provide them with scaffolding that will lead to new word learning. For example, when a Word Ladder clue indicates "Change one letter," you can provide support by specifying the letter in the word that needs to be changed. The activities in this book are too valuable to be used as independent seatwork. Rather, we hope you will use these activities to guide children to success and ever-higher levels of reading achievement.

This book (and its companion book for Grades 1–3) is designed to let children have fun reading and performing with friends, classmates, teachers, and family members. You can use this resource instructionally on-site, hybrid, or online, with the whole class, in small groups, at home, or in intervention settings to provide effective instruction and practice in reading. Poetry is known to engage striving or reluctant readers because of its use of rhyme, rhythm, and rich but limited-number vocabulary. Poems are also less intimidating to young readers and are meant to be rehearsed to improve fluency and confidence and to achieve success.

Ways to Extend Learning

In addition to the suggested lessons, you may wish to extend the experience by having children sort the featured words into various groups, such as:

- **grammatical categories**—e.g., words that are nouns and words that are not nouns
- **word structure**—e.g., words that have one syllable, two syllables, and three or more syllables; words that contain a long-vowel sound and words that contain a short-vowel sound; words that contain a consonant blend and words that do not
- **word meaning**—e.g., words that express what a person can do or feel and words that do not

This additional analysis through categorization will help children continue to analyze the words more deeply (orthographic mapping) and gain even greater control and understanding over them and related words. Extending examination of the featured phonogram (rime) in a Word Ladder and language arts lesson offers children engaging ways to expand their vocabulary.

Another way to extend children's word study is to choose, along with your students, some of the most interesting words from each Word Ladder activity and put them on display on a class word wall. Encourage children to read and refer to words on the word wall regularly and to use these words in their writing and conversation. And here's a tip about word walls: Put them at a height where they are easily accessible for student use. We often see word walls along the ceiling (where teachers probably have the most room), but this creates a transfer issue for some children as they try to look up and down to copy a word. Putting the words around the room where children can place a paper next to the needed word enables accurate and independent use of the words.

In today's focus on Social and Emotional Learning, we can think of no better vehicle for fostering community than using poetry for two or more voices. Such poems encourage working with others, which "increases student interest in learning, improves student behavior, prevents and reduces bullying, and improves school climate" (Bridgeland & Bruce, 2013). Regardless of how you deliver instruction, we hope you and your students will have fun with these phonograms!

Bonus Online Materials: To access printable templates and additional resources for this book, go to **www.scholastic.com/partnerpoemswordladders** and enter your email address and access code: **SC734191**.

Stop the Gab

1st Voice	All Together	2nd Voice
All my sister does is gab		
		gab gab gab gab
	gab gab gab gab	
yuck yuck		
		yuck yuck
	blab blab blab blab.	
She drives me crazy with her gab.		
		All day long it's gab gab.
There is no switch that I can grab,		
		no turn-off button I can jab,
no way to stop her		
	blab blab.	
All night long it's		
	gab gab.	
		My sister thinks it's cool to gab,
thinks it's neat,		
	thinks it's fab.	
		I'd pinch her if I were a crab—
	Anything to stop her gab!	

Name _____

Read the clues. Then, write the words.
Start at the bottom and climb to the top.

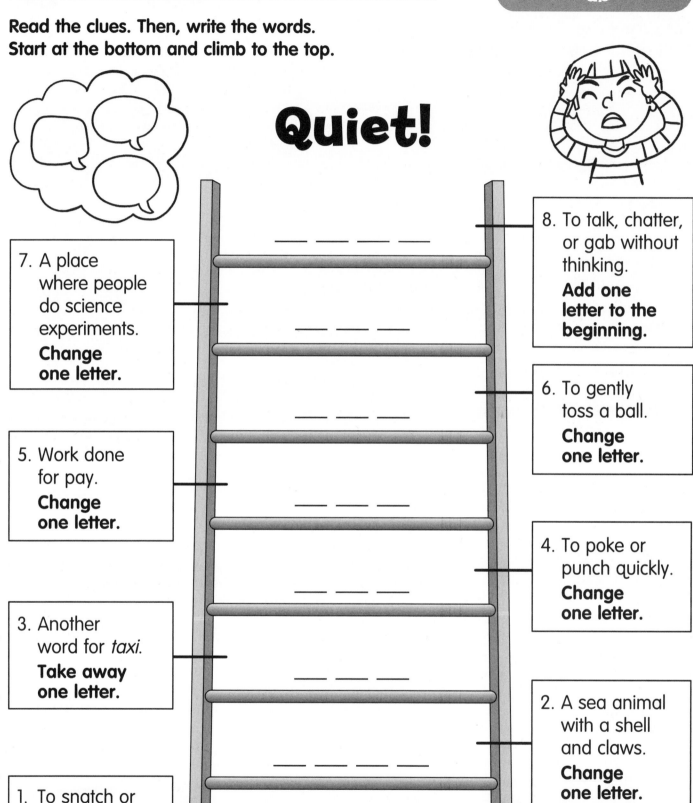

Quiet!

7. A place where people do science experiments. **Change one letter.**

5. Work done for pay. **Change one letter.**

3. Another word for *taxi*. **Take away one letter.**

1. To snatch or take hold of something. **Add one letter.**

8. To talk, chatter, or gab without thinking. **Add one letter to the beginning.**

6. To gently toss a ball. **Change one letter.**

4. To poke or punch quickly. **Change one letter.**

2. A sea animal with a shell and claws. **Change one letter.**

___ ___ ___ ___

___ ___ ___

___ ___ ___

___ ___ ___

___ ___ ___

___ ___ ___ ___

___ ___ ___

g a b

Partner Poems & Word Ladders for Building Foundational Literacy Skills: K–2 © by Harrison, Rasinski & Fresch, Scholastic Teaching Solutions

Name _____

Read the clues. Then, write the words.
Start at the bottom and climb to the top.

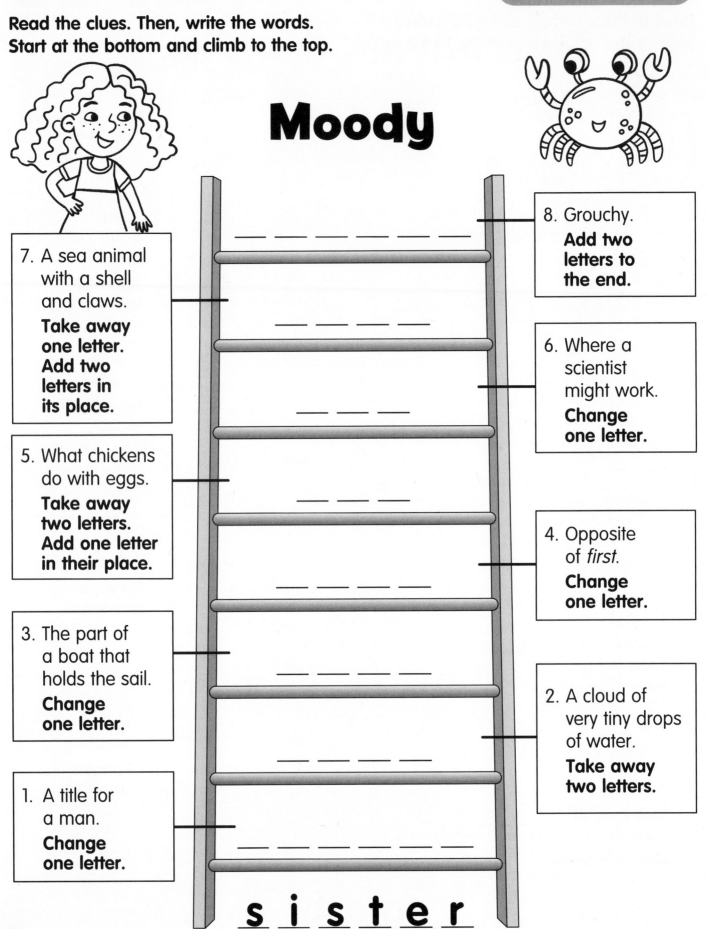

Moody

8. Grouchy.
Add two letters to the end.

7. A sea animal with a shell and claws.
Take away one letter. Add two letters in its place.

6. Where a scientist might work.
Change one letter.

5. What chickens do with eggs.
Take away two letters. Add one letter in their place.

4. Opposite of *first*.
Change one letter.

3. The part of a boat that holds the sail.
Change one letter.

2. A cloud of very tiny drops of water.
Take away two letters.

1. A title for a man.
Change one letter.

s i s t e r

Partner Poems & Word Ladders for Building Foundational Literacy Skills: K–2 © by Harrison, Rasinski & Fresch, Scholastic Teaching Solutions

Phonogram Grab Bag

Objective: Children will identify real words created by joining onset consonants with the *-ab* phonogram.

Materials

- "Stop the Gab" (page 12)
- Consonant Letter Cards (page 125)
- small bag or box (to put the consonant cards in)
- *-ab* phonogram printed on a square card for each child

-ab

Procedure

1. Invite children to read the poem aloud. Ask them to find the *-ab* words in the poem.

2. Give each child (or pair of children) an *-ab* phonogram card.

3. One at a time, ask children to draw a consonant card from the bag (or box).

4. Have them place the consonant card in front of their phonogram card and sound across the word.

5. Ask: *Does it make a real word?* If so, have them use the word in a sentence. If it does not make a real word, invite them to share one they know that contains *-ab*.

6. For more challenge, give children some consonant blend cards, such as *bl-, cr-, dr-, fl-, gr-, st-*.

-ab words		
cab	**blab**	abstract
dab	**crab**	baboon
fab	drab	cabinet
gab	flab	habit
jab	**grab**	habitat
lab	slab	rabid
nab	stab	tablet
tab		taboo

Assessment: How well does each child create a real word by combining the consonant and phonogram? Consider who may need more vocabulary experiences.

Partner Poems & Word Ladders for Building Foundational Literacy Skills: K–2 © by Harrison, Rasinski & Fresch, Scholastic Teaching Solutions

I Love My Yak

1st Voice

See my yak?

I named him Jack.

I love my yak.

Good old Jack.
I love my yak.

Pretty feathers,
pretty back,
pretty waddle,
pretty yak!

Jack's no yak?

Well, then . . .
I love my Jack,
the duck.

2nd Voice

That's no yak.

Jack's no yak.

Jack's no yak.
He has feathers
on his back.
Jack's no yak.

Jack has feathers
on his back.
He waddles with
a quack, quack.
Jack's no yak.

A yak is gray
or brown or black.
He has no feathers
down his back.
He doesn't waddle,
doesn't quack.
Jack's no yak!

No such luck.

Partner Poems & Word Ladders for Building Foundational Literacy Skills: K–2 © by Harrison, Rasinski & Fresch, Scholastic Teaching Solutions

Name _____

Read the clues. Then, write the words.
Start at the bottom and climb to the top.

Feathered Friend

7. Fast or speedy.
Change two letters.

5. Sound made by a chicken.
Take away the first letter. Add two letters in its place.

3. A short nail with a flat head.
Change one letter.

1. Another word for *one dollar*.
Change one letter.

8. Sound made by a duck.
Change one letter.

6. A short, sharp sound when you snap your fingers.
Change one letter.

4. To wrap someone in a blanket.
Change one letter.

2. Opposite of *front*.
Change one letter.

_ _ _ _ _

_ _ _ _ _

_ _ _ _ _

_ _ _ _ _

_ _ _ _

_ _ _ _

_ _ _ _

d u c k

Partner Poems & Word Ladders for Building Foundational Literacy Skills: K–2 © by Harrison, Rasinski & Fresch, Scholastic Teaching Solutions

Name _____

Read the clues. Then, write the words.
Start at the bottom and climb to the top.

My Pet Jack

8. A large wild ox that lives in Tibet. **Take away one letter.**

7. To talk without stopping. **Change one letter.**

6. To put away in a box. **Change one letter.**

5. To choose. **Take away two letters.**

4. A cucumber preserved in vinegar or salt water; it can be sweet or dill. **Change one letter.**

3. To poke or touch someone gently to make the person laugh. **Change one letter.**

2. To knock someone over in football. **Add two letters to the end.**

1. A short nail with a flat head. **Change one letter.**

_ _ _ _

_ _ _ _ _

_ _ _ _ _

_ _ _ _ _

_ _ _ _ _ _

_ _ _ _ _

_ _ _ _ _

_ _ _ _

J a c k

18

Noun, Verb, Adjective

Objective: Children will categorize *-ack* words as noun (person/place), verb (action word), or adjective (descriptive word).

Materials

- "I Love My Yak" (page 16)
- 10 blank 3-by-3-inch cards (per child or pair of children)
- blank sheet of paper (per child or pair of children)

Procedure

1. Invite children to read the poem aloud. Have them find the *-ack* words in the poem.

2. Give each child 10 blank cards and a blank sheet of paper. Have children divide the sheet of paper into thirds. Ask them to label the columns "Noun," "Verb," and "Adjective."

3. Invite a child to read aloud an *-ack* word from the poem (*Jack, back, quack, black*). Have children write that word on a blank card. Repeat with the other three words.

4. Have children place each card in the proper column. (**noun:** *Jack, back*; **verb:** *quack*; **adjective:** *black*)

5. Ask children to think of four more *-ack* words to write on four of the remaining cards. (See list at right.) Then have them place the word cards in the proper column.

6. Have children choose any two words from the poem and write them on the remaining cards. Then have them place each card in the proper column. (**noun:** *yak, feathers, luck, duck*; **verb:** *see, named, love, has, waddles, is, doesn't*; **adjective:** *good, old, pretty, gray, brown, down*)

-ack words		
back	**black**	attack
hack	clack	cackle
Jack	crack	cracker
lack	flack	jackal
pack	knack	jacket
quack	shack	packet
rack	slack	racket
sack	smack	tackle
	snack	unpack
	stack	
	track	
	whack	

Assessment: Could children properly identify nouns, verbs, and adjectives? Could they think of four other *-ack* words? Could they find other nouns, verbs, and adjectives in the poem? Answers will provide insight into their understandings of how words are categorized in English.

Wondering about *yak*?

Yak certainly sounds like the other words in this poem. We know "ck" follows a short-vowel sound (such as *back*; words with a long-vowel sound end in "k"—such as *peek*). So what about *yak*? We turn to the word's origin. *Yak* is an English version of a Tibetan word—*g-yag*—which means "wild ox of Central Asia." English adopted the word.

You Need a Bag

1st Voice

I'm telling you, you need a bag.

To put stuff in.

Sure, to carry, or even drag.

Right, but careful not to snag
your put-stuff-in-carry-or-drag bag.

Don't wish to brag,
but once I turned my
put-stuff-in-carry-or-drag-
don't-snag bag
into a rag-flag with a leaping stag.

Yes, you do,
I'm telling you.
But, of course,
I hate to nag.

2nd Voice

Why would I ever need a bag?

A put-stuff-in bag?

**So you say I need a
put-stuff-in-carry-or-drag bag.**

**You worry too much.
I won't snag my
put-stuff-in-carry-or-drag bag.**

**I don't need a
rag-flag-stag bag.
And I don't need a
put-stuff-in-carry-or-drag-
don't-snag bag.**

Partner Poems & Word Ladders for Building Foundational Literacy Skills: K–2 © by Harrison, Rasinski & Fresch, Scholastic Teaching Solutions

Name _____

**Read the clues. Then, write the words.
Start at the bottom and climb to the top.**

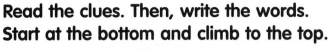

Grab Bag

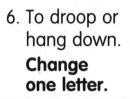

7. To complain all the time.
Change one letter.

____ ____ ____

6. To droop or hang down.
Change one letter.

____ ____ ____

5. An outdoor game played by children.
Change one letter.

____ ____ ____

4. A cloth used for cleaning.
Change one letter.

____ ____ ____

3. To move a tail back and forth like a dog.
Change one letter.

____ ____ ____

2. Fake hair worn on the head.
Change one letter.

____ ____ ____

1. Opposite of *small*.
Change one letter.

____ ____ ____

b a g

Name _____

Read the clues. Then, write the words.
Start at the bottom and climb to the top.

Lots of Stuff

7. My teacher has a "___ of tricks" to help us learn.
Take away one letter.

6. To boast about how good you are.
Change two letters.

5. A male deer.
Add a letter to the beginning.

4. A game kids play.
Change one letter.

3. To pull hard.
Take away two letters. Add one letter in their place.

2. To put a child to bed and cover snugly.
Take away one letter.

1. When something is glued in place, it's ___.
Change the last two letters.

— — — (7)

— — — — (6)

— — — (5)

— — — — (4)

— — — (3)

— — — — (2)

— — — — (1)

__s__ __t__ __u__ __f__ __f__

Partner Poems & Word Ladders for Building Foundational Literacy Skills: K–2 © by Harrison, Rasinski & Fresch, Scholastic Teaching Solutions

Sequencing Cumulative Events

Objective: Children will sequence the cumulative events in the poem.

Materials
- "You Need a Bag" (page 20)
- scissors

Procedure

1. Make a photocopy of the poem for each pair of children. Cut apart the poem into the 11 1st Voice and 2nd Voice stanzas. Be sure to keep the multiple lines for each voice together.

2. Have children take turns reading the 1st Voice and 2nd Voice several times. This poem builds in cumulative events. (Cumulative events rely on considering what has been added each time to the poem, similar to "This Is the House That Jack Built.")

3. Pair up children and give the cut stanzas to partners. You might keep the first stanza ("I'm telling you, you need a bag") to start the poem.

-ag words		
bag	**brag**	baggy
gag	**drag**	dagger
hag	**flag**	dragon
lag	**snag**	haggle
nag	**stag**	jagged
rag		magma
sag		maggot
tag		magpie
wag		ragtag
zag		saggy
		wagon

4. Read aloud the first line. Ask the children to look at the stanzas they have. What comes next? How do you know? Have partners work together to rebuild the poem.

Assessment: Observe who contributes to the event building. Do children understand that more is added with each stanza? To review, show the entire poem and give children the opportunity to sort their stanzas into the correct order.

Run, Meg, Run!

1st Voice

Pam went down to the barn one day,

to the pen of a hen she called Meg.

"I'm here to ask you, Meg," said Pam,

"if you would please lay me an egg."

Now, Meg was a hen
and a very smart hen.

She knew why Pam wanted her egg.

She cooked up a plan
and decided to scram

or Pam would soon scramble her egg.

Good plan.

How?

Hmm . . .

Smart!
Pam told herself that her chicken
had fled.

"No egg for my dinner," she said.

She settled for crackers and jam

and a watercress salad with yam.

2nd Voice

Why?

"Hi, Meg!"

Uh-oh . . .

Oh, no!

Think, Meg!

I can't look.

Run, Meg, run!

Oh, yuck!

She hopped in the barn and
hid with the sheep.

"Hide me!" she clucked to the ram.

The ram knew that Pam was
allergic to wool,

so he dressed Meg to look
like a lamb,

Whew.

Poor Pam.

Awwww.

Yay, Meg!

Name _____

**Read the clues. Then, write the words.
Start at the bottom and climb to the top.**

Meg in a Jam

7. A sweet spread made by cooking crushed fruit and sugar.
Take away two letters. Add one letter in their place.

— — —

8. The name of the girl in the story.
Change one letter.

— — —

6. To fill or stuff something with more than it can hold.
Take away one letter.

— — — —

5. To get out or go away immediately.
Add two letters to the beginning.

— — — — —

4. A male sheep.
Change one letter.

— — —

3. "Today, I will run two miles. Yesterday, I ___ one mile."
Change one letter.

— — —

2. When a boy grows up, he becomes a ___.
Change one letter.

— — —

1. Boys grow up to be these.
Change one letter.

— — —

M e g

Name _____

Read the clues. Then, write the words.
Start at the bottom and climb to the top.

Snack Time

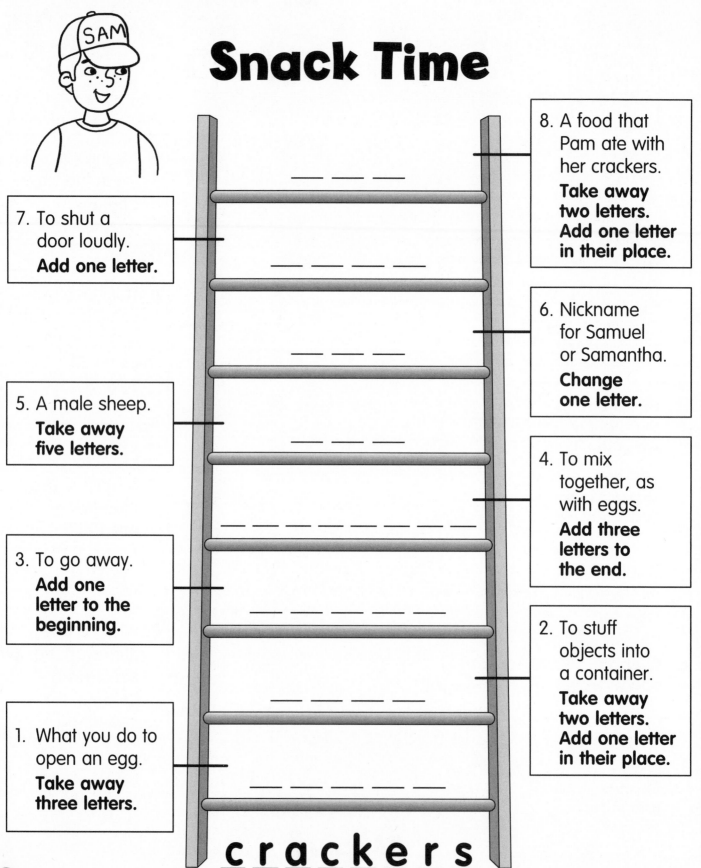

7. To shut a door loudly. **Add one letter.**

5. A male sheep. **Take away five letters.**

3. To go away. **Add one letter to the beginning.**

1. What you do to open an egg. **Take away three letters.**

8. A food that Pam ate with her crackers. **Take away two letters. Add one letter in their place.**

6. Nickname for Samuel or Samantha. **Change one letter.**

4. To mix together, as with eggs. **Add three letters to the end.**

2. To stuff objects into a container. **Take away two letters. Add one letter in their place.**

c r a c k e r s

Alphabetical Order

Objective: Children will alphabetize the *-am* words.

Materials

- "Run, Meg, Run!" (page 24)
- highlighters
- 2 strips of paper for each pair of children (Cut a sheet of paper in half lengthwise.)
- scissors

Procedure

1. Invite children to read the poem aloud.

2. Pair up children to work together to highlight the *-am* words in the poem.

3. Next, have children write the *-am* words on the first strip of paper, then cut the words apart. Ask them to put the words in ABC (alphabetical) order.

4. Challenge partners to think of other *-am* words and write them on the second strip of paper. Use the list at right to give clues if they get stuck on ideas for words. (For example, *Yesterday we jumped in the pool and _____.*) For children who are ready, provide clues to more complex words. (For example, *This is a panda's favorite food.*)

5. After children have finished making their second list of words, have them cut the words apart. Then have them add the new words to their alphabetized list, moving slips to provide space for them.

-am words		
am	blam	amble
bam	clam	bamboo
dam	cram	camp
ham	gram	clammy
jam	ma'am	cramp
lam	**scram**	damage
Pam	sham	exam
ram	slam	hamper
Sam	spam	**lamb**
tam	swam	pamper
yam	wham	ramp
		scramble
		shampoo
		webcam

Assessment: Do children understand what it means to put words in alphabetical order? Do you need to review/reteach this skill? Observe the words children created for their second strip.

Wondering about *lamb*?

Although *lamb* rhymes with the other *-am* words in the poem, it ends with the silent *b*. Words like *lamb* are from long ago, and at one time the /b/ sound was pronounced. Over time English speakers changed the pronunciation of these words to end with the /m/ sound but did not change the spelling. Challenge children to think of other words that end in the silent "b" (*tomb, numb, limb, comb, thumb*). Sometimes we hear the /b/ sound in related words (*bombard, crumble*).

Fix the Fan

1st Voice

It's hot in here!
Turn on the fan.

Last night it ran.
What do we do?

Call a man
to fix the fan.

Hey, Ann.
Please fix the fan.

Fran, who drives
the fix-it van?

It's me, Fran.
I can't fix this fan.
You need to buy
a part from Dan.

"I plugged it in,"
said Jan.

2nd Voice

The fan won't work.

We need a plan.

Don't need a man
to fix the fan.
Ann can.

I tried but I
can't fix the fan.
Call Fran.

The tan van.
Call Fran.

Hey, someone
fixed the fan!

Partner Poems & Word Ladders for Building Foundational Literacy Skills: K–2 © by Harrison, Parinski & Frosch Scholastic Teaching Solutions

Name _____

Read the clues. Then, write the words.
Start at the bottom and climb to the top.

Ride On!

7. A yellowish-brown color.
Change one letter.

___ ___ ___

6. A game children play.
Change one letter.

___ ___ ___

5. A sack for holding things.
Change one letter.

___ ___ ___

4. An old cloth used for cleaning.
Change one letter.

___ ___ ___

3. "Today I will run farther than I ___ yesterday."
Change one letter.

___ ___ ___

2. Someone who enjoys a particular sport, game, or pastime.
Change one letter.

___ ___ ___

1. An adult male.
Change one letter.

___ ___ ___

v a n

29

Name _____

Read the clues. Then, write the words.
Start at the bottom and climb to the top.

Fix It, Please!

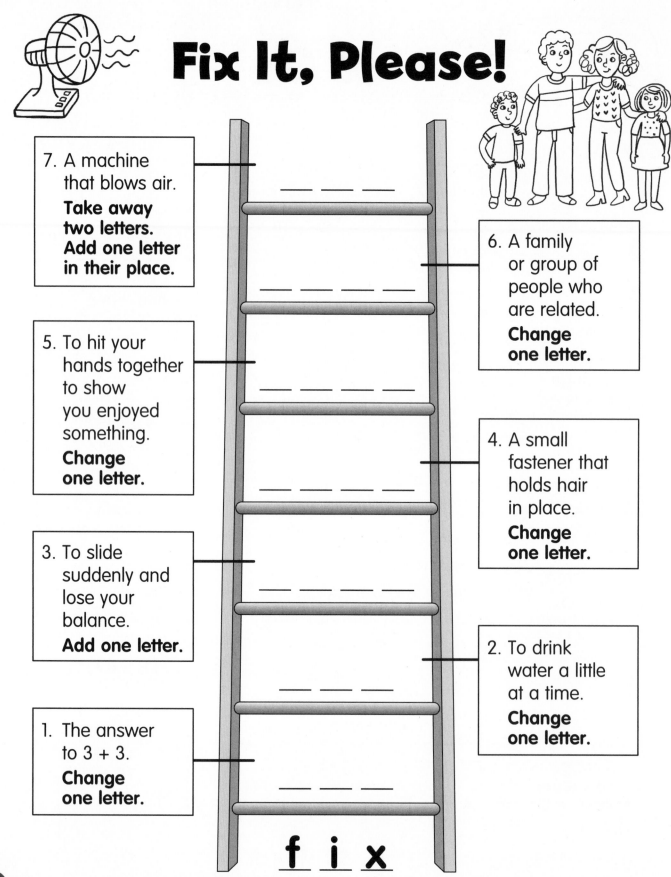

7. A machine that blows air.
Take away two letters. Add one letter in their place.

_ _ _ _

6. A family or group of people who are related.
Change one letter.

_ _ _ _

5. To hit your hands together to show you enjoyed something.
Change one letter.

_ _ _ _

4. A small fastener that holds hair in place.
Change one letter.

_ _ _ _

3. To slide suddenly and lose your balance.
Add one letter.

_ _ _ _

2. To drink water a little at a time.
Change one letter.

_ _ _ _

1. The answer to 3 + 3.
Change one letter.

_ _ _ _

f i x

Fortunately, Unfortunately

Objective: Children will recognize "Fortunately, Unfortunately" statements in the poem and write their own.

Materials
- "Fix the Fan" (page 28)
- "Fortunately, Unfortunately" sentence starters (see below)

Procedure

1. Invite the class to read the poem aloud. Have children take turns reading 1st Voice and 2nd Voice.

2. After several readings, show children how to turn the events in the poem into "Fortunately, Unfortunately" statements. Write the words *Fortunately* and *Unfortunately* on the board and discuss their meaning. (*Fortunately* means "luckily" and *unfortunately* means "unluckily or sadly.")

3. Guide children to create the following statements:

   Fortunately, we have a fan, because it's hot.

   Unfortunately, the fan did not work.

   Fortunately, last night the fan ran.

   Unfortunately, we need a plan.

   Fortunately, we can call someone to fix the fan.

   Unfortunately, Ann can't fix the fan.

   Fortunately, Fran in the tan fix-it van can come.

   Unfortunately, Fran can't fix it; we need to call Dan for a part.

   Fortunately, the fan worked! Jan plugged it in.

-*an* words		
an	bran	**Ann**
ban	clan	antics
can	**Fran**	bland
Dan	**plan**	brand
fan	scan	canny
Jan	span	canvas
man	Stan	canyon
pan		chant
ran		dandy
tan		manor
van		panda
		sand
		sandy

4. Pair up children and have partners try to create their own "Fortunately, Unfortunately" statements. If necessary, give a starter, such as:

   Fortunately, it was Saturday. Unfortunately, _____.

   Fortunately, it was lunchtime. Unfortunately, _____.

   Fortunately, I studied for the test. Unfortunately, _____.

Assessment: Observe children as they try to decide which events are fortunate and unfortunate. Do they apply that understanding to their own sentences?

The Sea of Rank

1st Voice

2nd Voice

3rd Voice

Fishes come,
fishes go
in the ancient
Sea of Rank.

They say
long, long ago,
a ship of pirates sank.

*They say the pirates
chained their prisoners
to hear them cry and clank,*

then laughed, "Bye-bye!"
and made their prisoners
sigh and walk the plank.

Fishes come,
fishes go
in the ancient
Sea of Rank.

The pirates' ship
was dark and dank.
With a "Yo-ho-ho!"
they drank and stank!

*Till the King's Navy
with cannonballs
made sure
those pirates sank.*

Fishes come,
fishes go
in the ancient
Sea of Rank.

Name _____

**Read the clues. Then, write the words.
Start at the bottom and climb to the top.**

By the Sea

8. To put things in order, like shortest to tallest. Also, the name of the sea in the story. **Change one letter.**

_ _ _ _ _

7. A place where you keep your money safe. **Take away one letter.**

_ _ _ _

6. An empty line or space. **Change one letter.**

_ _ _ _ _

5. The sound made by a piece of metal hitting another. **Take away one letter. Add two letters in its place.**

_ _ _ _ _

4. A large container for storing liquids, such as water. **Add one letter to the end.**

_ _ _ _

3. A light brown color. **Change one letter.**

_ _ _

2. The answer to 9 + 1. **Change one letter.**

_ _ _

1. A hot drink; it can also be iced. **Change one letter.**

_ _ _

s e a

Read the clues. Then, write the words.
Start at the bottom and climb to the top.

Ahoy, There!

7. What you do with your legs. Also, what pirates make prisoners do on a plank. **Take away two letters. Add one letter in their place.**

_ _ _ _ _

6. The main stem of a plant. **Add one letter to the beginning.**

_ _ _ _ _

5. To speak with someone. **Change one letter.**

_ _ _ _ _

4. An armored vehicle with a large gun. **Change one letter.**

_ _ _ _ _

3. A place where people keep money. **Change one letter.**

_ _ _ _ _

2. An official position in the military, such as general. **Take away one letter.**

_ _ _ _ _

1. A trick that is played on someone. **Change one letter.**

_ _ _ _ _

plank

Word Wheel

Objective: Children will create a word wheel with *-ank* words.

Materials

- "The Sea of Rank" (page 32)
- Consonant Letter and Cluster Cards (pages 125–127)
- scissors
- 9-inch round paper plates
- glue
- paper fastener/brad
- 7-by-2-inch strips of cardboard
- paper

Procedure

1. Invite children to read the poem aloud. Ask them to find the *-ank* words in the poem.

2. Have children cut apart the Consonant Letter and Cluster Cards. Have them mix up the cards together.

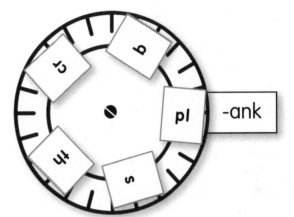

3. To make the word wheel, provide each child with a paper plate. Have children lay as many of the consonant cards as will fit around the outer edge of the plate (see above). Then, have them glue the consonant cards in place.

4. Give each child a strip of cardboard and assist children to push the fastener through the plate and strip. (Alternatively, you can assemble the plate and strip ahead of time.) Have children write *ank* on the part of the strip that is sticking out.

5. To use the word wheel, have children turn the paper plate and see if the consonant letter or blend combined with *-ank* makes a word. Remind them to blend the letters on the plate with the phonogram *-ank*.

6. If children make a word, have them write it on a sheet of paper. You can have partners work together to turn the wheel and check if they have a real word. Examples of words are at right.

Assessment: Check the words created by the children. Are they all real words? If there are any that are not (for instance, *jank*), ask children to sound it out for you. They may be able to sound it out correctly, so ask if they can use it in a sentence. Then, discuss any that are not real words (but they may have sounded out correctly).

-ank words		
bank	blank	ankle
dank	**clank**	bankrupt
Hank	crank	blanket
rank	**drank**	clanked
sank	flank	cranky
tank	Frank	embankment
yank	**plank**	hanky
	shank	lanky
	spank	plankton
	stank	swanky
	swank	tanker
	thank	thankful

What Do You Do?

1st Voice	**All Together**	**2nd Voice**

All Together

What do you do
when the cold winds blow?

1st Voice

I'm an indoor chap.
I spread a wrap
across my lap.

2nd Voice

I'm an outdoor chap.
I wear a cap
and grab a map.

All Together

And what do you do
when the cold winds blow
and there's ice and snow?

1st Voice

Ice and snow?

2nd Voice

Ice and snow?

All Together

Ice and snow.

1st Voice

I spread a wrap
across my lap
and read and nap
by the fire's glow.

2nd Voice

I wear a cap,
grab a map,
a critter trap,
and off I go.

(continued)

1st Voice

All Together

2nd Voice

**But what do you do
when the cold winds blow,
there's ice and snow,
and it's ten below?**

Ten below?

Ten below?

Ten below.

*I take off my cap,
fold my map,
store the trap,
spread a wrap
across my lap,
and read and nap
by the fire's glow.
That's what I do.*

What about you?

Name _____

**Read the clues. Then, write the words.
Start at the bottom and climb to the top.**

Head Wear

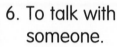

7. Something worn on the head, like a cap.
Take away one letter.

6. To talk with someone.
Change one letter.

5. To become rough or dry, especially skin. Also, a male friend.
Change one letter.

4. To hit your hands together to show you liked something.
Change one letter.

3. What birds do with their wings to fly.
Add one letter to the beginning.

2. When sitting, the part of the body between the knees and hips.
Change one letter.

1. A liquid that comes out of many trees in the spring.
Change one letter.

c a p

Partner Poems & Word Ladders for Building Foundational Literacy Skills: K–2 © by Harrison, Rasinski & Fresch, Scholastic Teaching Solutions

Name _____

Read the clues. Then, write the words.
Start at the bottom and climb to the top.

Staying In

7. The winner of a competition. Short for *champion*.
Change one letter.

5. Noise made by hitting the hands together quickly.
Take away the first letter. Add two letters in its place.

3. Something used for frying foods.
Change one letter.

1. Opposite of *out*.
Take away four letters.

8. A male friend.
Take away one letter.

6. A tool for holding things together.
Add one letter.

4. To sleep for a short time.
Move the letters around.

2. "Mom will ___ my medal on my shirt."
Add one letter.

i n d o o r

Partner Poems & Word Ladders for Building Foundational Literacy Skills: K–2 © by Harrison, Rasinski & Fresch, Scholastic Teaching Solutions

Bingo

Objective: Children will write *-ap* words on a bingo game card and then identify the words as they play the game.

Materials

- "What Do You Do?" (page 36)
- blank 5-by-5 bingo grid for each child (see right)
- pencils
- bingo markers (or beans or pennies)

Procedure

1. Invite children to read the poem aloud. Have them find the *-ap* words in the poem.

2. Distribute blank bingo grids and pencils to children.

3. Read aloud the words in the first and second columns of the chart below. Ask children to write each word on any square on their grid.

4. Choose three additional words from the third column.

5. To play, give children markers for covering words on their bingo grid. Randomly call out a word from the list and have children cover that word on their grid. Continue until a player has covered five words in a row—across, down, or diagonally. Have the player read aloud the words covered.

6. Continue to play to let more children get bingo.

Assessment: Observe as children write the words. Do they need assistance? Did the children who called "bingo" cover the correct words?

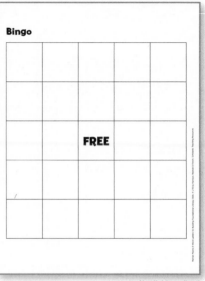

(Available online.)

-ap words		
cap	**chap**	burlap
gap	clap	capitol
hap	flap	captain
lap	scrap	capture
map	slap	entrap
nap	snap	flapper
rap	strap	happy
sap	**trap**	icecap
tap	whap	lapdog
yap	**wrap**	scrappy
zap		uncap
		unsnap

Partner Poems & Word Ladders for Building Foundational Literacy Skills: K–2 © by Harrison, Rasinski & Fresch, Scholastic Teaching Solutions

The Gnat's Hat

1st Voice

There was a gnat.

There was a bat
who saw the gnat
who wore a hat.

There was a rat
who saw the bat
who ate the gnat
who wore a hat.

There was a cat
who saw the rat
who ate the bat
who ate the gnat
who wore a hat.

2nd Voice

There was a gnat
who wore a hat.

Said the bat,
"I'll eat the gnat,
but not her hat.
I do not like
the gnat's hat."

Said the rat,
"I'll eat the bat
who ate the gnat
who wore a hat,
but not her hat.
I do not like
the gnat's hat."

Said the cat,
"I'll eat the rat
who ate the bat
who ate the gnat.
I love her hat!"
And off he went
in the gnat's hat.

Partner Poems & Word Ladders for Building Foundational Literacy Skills: K–2 © by Harrison, Rasinski & Fresch, Scholastic Teaching Solutions

Name _____

**Read the clues. Then, write the words.
Start at the bottom and climb to the top.**

It's on Your Head

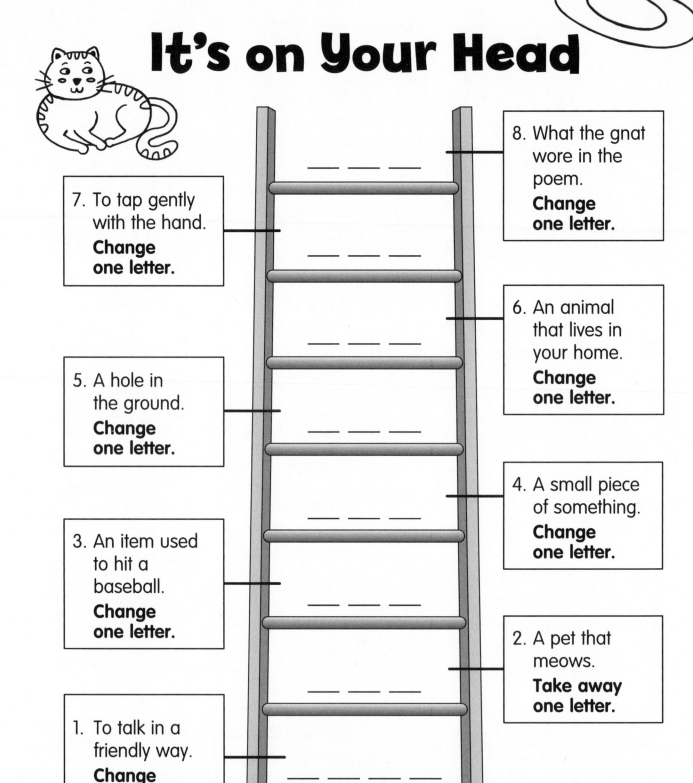

8. What the gnat wore in the poem.
Change one letter.

7. To tap gently with the hand.
Change one letter.

6. An animal that lives in your home.
Change one letter.

5. A hole in the ground.
Change one letter.

4. A small piece of something.
Change one letter.

3. An item used to hit a baseball.
Change one letter.

2. A pet that meows.
Take away one letter.

1. To talk in a friendly way.
Change two letters.

_ _ _ _

g n a t

Partner Poems & Word Ladders for Building Foundational Literacy Skills: K–2 © by Harrison, Rasinski & Fresch, Scholastic Teaching Solutions

Name _____

Read the clues. Then, write the words.
Start at the bottom and climb to the top.

Furry Pets

8. A pet animal that barks. **Change one letter.**

7. What you do with a shovel. **Change one letter.**

6. Another word for *large*. **Change one letter.**

5. A sack used for carrying things. **Change one letter.**

4. An animal with wings but is not a bird. **Change one letter.**

3. An animal that looks like a large mouse. **Take away three letters.**

2. A noisy toy for babies. **Change one letter.**

1. A group of cows. **Add three letters to the end.**

c a t

Dramatize the Poem

Objective: Children will show comprehension of the poem by dramatizing the sequence of events.

Materials

- "The Gnat's Hat" (page 41)
- signs or name tags with each character's name (*Gnat, Bat, Rat, Cat*)
- child's hat

Procedure

1. Have children practice reading the poem with a partner a few times so they are familiar with the events. Circulate as they read to listen for any needed assistance.

2. Choose four children to play the parts of the characters. Provide each child with a sign or name tag with the character's name. Give the Gnat a hat to wear.

3. Divide the class in half. Have half of the class read aloud 1st Voice and the other half read 2nd Voice.

4. As the class reads the poem, have the four children act out their character's part.

5. Repeat so each child in the class has the opportunity to play one of the characters.

-at words		
at	blat	battery
bat	brat	catfish
cat	drat	democrat
fat	flat	format
hat	frat	habitat
mat	**gnat**	latitude
pat	slat	platform
rat	spat	scratch
sat	splat	statue
vat	sprat	

Assessment: Listen as children read aloud the poem the first time. Do they stumble on any of the words? Consider how you might support children who need assistance during the first readings.

Partner Poems & Word Ladders for Building Foundational Literacy Skills: K–2 © by Harrison, Rasinski & Fresch, Scholastic Teaching Solutions

The Missing Donkey

1st Voice	All Together	2nd Voice

All Together

**The day was cool,
cloudy,
gray.**

1st Voice

Out in the barn
in the donkey's bay,
Farmer found only
a cat and some hay.

2nd Voice

He kicked the hay
and chased the cat.
How could a donkey
disappear like that?

How did his donkey
get away?
Farmer didn't know
what to say.

**The day was cool
cloudy,
gray.**

He looked outside
for tracks in the clay.

The wind was strong.
It made him sway.
He listened for
his donkey's bray.

All he heard,
was a loud blue jay.
Could a thief have stolen
his donkey away?

**The day was cool,
cloudy,
gray.**

(continued)

1st Voice

He said, "I'll find
that thief some way.
I'll find that thief
and make him pay!"

Could it be his donkey?

Louder and louder,
it headed his way
till Farmer learned
   something
important that day.

Instead of one donkey,
now Farmer had two!
Farmer was happy,
and his donkey was too.

All Together

The day was cool,
cloudy,
gray,
but the farmer's story
ends well.
Hooray!

2nd Voice

*Just then he heard
from far away
a sound he knew—
a donkey's bray!*

*Hard to say.
It came from the water,
down by the bay.*

*No thief had taken
his donkey away.
His donkey had left
on his own to go play!*

Name _____

**Read the clues. Then, write the words.
Start at the bottom and climb to the top.**

Cloudy Day

7. Color often used to describe cloudy days.
Change one letter.

_ _ _ _

6. To take hold of something.
Add one letter.

_ _ _ _

5. To talk or chat without thinking.
Change one letter.

_ _ _

4. Cheerful or jolly.
Change one letter.

_ _ _

3. Money earned for working.
Take away one letter.

_ _ _

2. What children do on a playground.
Change one letter.

1. A kind of earthy material used to make pottery.
Take away "oud." Add one letter in their place.

_ _ _ _

_ _ _ _

c l o u d y

47

Name _____

**Read the clues. Then, write the words.
Start at the bottom and climb to the top.**

Donkey Says...

8. Sound made by a donkey. **Add one letter.**

7. An inlet or cove of water near the edge of the sea. **Change one letter.**

6. A young male. **Change one letter.**

5. An object used for play. **Change one letter.**

4. A weight of 2,000 pounds. **Add one letter.**

3. Opposite of *off*. **Take away three letters.**

2. Dollars and cents are examples of this. **Take away one letter.**

1. A furry animal with a long tail that likes to climb trees. **Change one letter.**

d o n k e y

Partner Poems & Word Ladders for Building Foundational Literacy Skills: K–2 © by Harrison, Rasinski & Fresch, Scholastic Teaching Solutions

Sorting Words

Objective: Children will discern differences in the phonogram by separating single consonant onsets (*d-ay, s-ay*) from consonant blend onsets (*br-ay, gr-ay*).

Materials

- "The Missing Donkey" (page 45)
- Consonant Sorting Chart (see right), copied or projected for whole class, individual, or partner work

Procedure

1. Invite the class to read the poem aloud. You can have individual children or partners read the 1st Voice and 2nd Voice, while the rest of the class reads the All Together voice.

2. Ask children to help create a list of all the words in the poem that contain *-ay*. (*day, gray, bay, hay, away, say, clay, sway, bray, jay, way, pay, play, hooray*) Write these words on the board or on chart paper for all children to refer to as they begin the sorting activity.

3. Call on volunteers to write the words under the correct heading.

   - Words that start with a single consonant: *day, bay, hay, say, jay, way, pay*
   - Words that start with a consonant blend: *gray, clay, sway, bray, play*
   - Words that make us think: *away, hooray*

4. Ask children to think of any words they know that contain *-ay* but were not in the poem. Where would they place those words in the sorting chart? Are they single consonant onsets (e.g., *lay, ray, may*) or consonant blends (e.g., *pray, spray, stay, tray*)? Are there other words that make us think? (e.g., *x-ray, replay, decay*)

5. Ask children to choose two or more of the words to create their own two-sentence rhyme.

Assessment: Evaluate how well children could sort the *-ay* words into the correct columns. Do they sort the words correctly? Evaluate if they are able to add any other words to the chart. Are they able to think of any other *-ay* words?

Consonant Sorting Chart

Words that start with a single consonant	Words that start with a consonant blend	Words that make us think*

* **Note:** "Words that make us think" is a place for words that don't exactly sort into one of the other two columns but fit the phonogram pattern.

-ay words		
bay	**bray**	away
day	**clay**	decay
gay	cray	defray
hay	**gray**	delay
jay	**play**	everyday
lay	pray	holiday
may	slay	**hooray**
pay	stay	moray
ray	**sway**	okay
say	tray	roadway
way		stowaway

Lazy Fred

1st Voice

Ted went sliding
on his sled.

Ted painted
his roof red.

Ted sawed wood
and built a shed.

Ted fell in love
and soon was wed.

2nd Voice

Lazy Fred?
Stayed in bed.

Meanwhile, Fred?
Stayed in bed.

Fred? As usual,
stayed in bed.

Fred wished
to be like Ted,
but instead,
stayed in bed.

Partner Poems & Word Ladders for Building Foundational Literacy Skills: K–2 © by Harrison, Rasinski & Fresch, Scholastic Teaching Solutions

Name _____

Read the clues. Then, write the words.
Start at the bottom and climb to the top.

Fred and Friend

8. Fred's friend in the poem. **Change one letter.**

7. You sleep on this. **Change one letter.**

6. Opposite of *good*. **Change one letter.**

5. To offer an amount of money to buy something. **Change one letter.**

4. The cover of a jar. **Take away one letter.**

3. "We ___ across the ice on the rink." **Change one letter.**

2. Something you ride on the snow. **Take away one letter. Add two letters in its place.**

1. A color. **Take away one letter.**

F r e d

Partner Poems & Word Ladders for Building Foundational Literacy Skills: K–2 © by Harrison, Rasinski & Fresch, Scholastic Teaching Solutions

Name _____

Read the clues. Then, write the words.
Start at the bottom and climb to the top.

The Color of Love

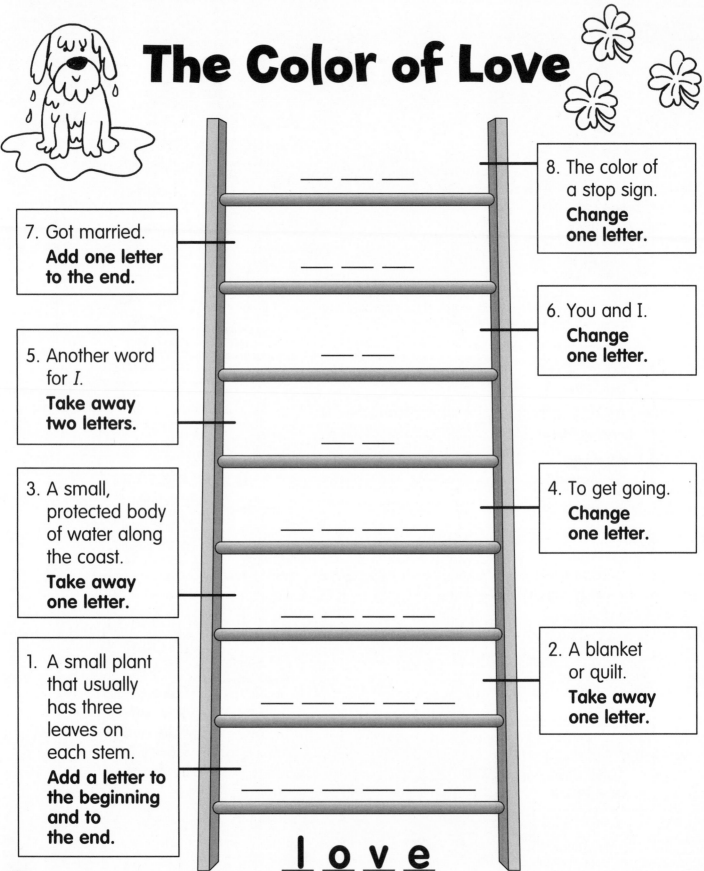

— — — —

7. Got married.
**Add one letter
to the end.**

8. The color of
a stop sign.
**Change
one letter.**

— — — —

5. Another word
for *I*.
**Take away
two letters.**

6. You and I.
**Change
one letter.**

— —

— —

3. A small,
protected body
of water along
the coast.
**Take away
one letter.**

4. To get going.
**Change
one letter.**

— — — —

— — — —

1. A small plant
that usually
has three
leaves on
each stem.
**Add a letter to
the beginning
and to
the end.**

2. A blanket
or quilt.
**Take away
one letter.**

— — — — —

— — — — —

l o v e

Partner Poems & Word Ladders for Building Foundational Literacy Skills: K–2 © by Harrison, Rasinski & Fresch, Scholastic Teaching Solutions

Sequence of Events

Objective: Children will write a story using the events from the poem.

Materials

- "Lazy Fred" (page 50)
- writing paper

Procedure

1. Pair up children and have partners read the poem several times to be certain they know the sequence of events in the poem.

2. Together, ask children to help you complete this outline (project or copy onto chart paper):

   a. First, Ted _____

   b. But Fred _____

   c. Next, Ted _____

   d. But Fred _____

   e. Then, Ted _____

   f. But Fred _____

   g. Finally, Ted _____

   h. And Fred _____

-ed words		
bed	bled	credible
fed	bred	edition
led	fled	editor
red	**Fred**	federal
Ted	pled	hundred
wed	**shed**	medicine
	shred	tragedy
	sled	
	sped	

3. Invite children to help you find and highlight all the *-ed* words in the poem. *(Ted, sled, Fred, bed, red, shed, wed)* Ask: *What other -ed words do you know?*

Assessment: Do children successfully contribute to the sequence of events? Are any children unable to assist in the activity? Further experiences with sequencing may be beneficial for these children. For example, you might print out sentences from the poem and cut them apart for individualized practice.

Our Hero Jill

1st Voice

Once upon a windy hill
lived a little girl named Jill.
Jill had brothers, Bill and Phil.

2nd Voice

A dragon lived below the hill.
Its hiss was loud, its scream was shrill.
The dragon frightened Bill and Phil.

"Nothing frightens me," said Jill.

One windy day, wet and chill,
the dragon captured Bill and Phil.
"I'll barbecue you on my grill,"
the dragon laughed, "and have my fill."
He seasoned them with salt and dill.
"While I eat you, please lie still."

The boys were done for sure, until
down the hill came sister Jill,
who used her dragon-talking skill.
"Those boys," she said, "will make you ill!"

The dragon rattled scales at Jill.
"What do you mean, they'll make
   me ill?"

"Bill's a brat, and Phil's a pill,"
she told the dragon under the hill.
"A brat and a pill will make you ill."

Ill at the thought of being ill,
he took the brothers off the grill
and dived in a hole beneath the hill.

And that's how Jill saved Bill and Phil.

Partner Poems & Word Ladders for Building Foundational Literacy Skills: K–2 © by Harrison Reginski & French Scholastic Teaching Solutions

Name _____

Read the clues. Then, write the words.
Start at the bottom and climb to the top.

She's Got Skill

8. Bill's sister
in the poem.
**Change
one letter.**

7. An annoying
person. Also,
a small, solid
medicine taken
by mouth.
**Take away
one letter.**

6. To let a liquid
run out of
a container.
**Change
one letter.**

5. Quiet; without
moving.
**Change
one letter.**

4. Part of a stable
where a horse
is kept.
**Change
one letter.**

3. Opposite
of *large*.
**Add one
letter to the
beginning.**

2. A large indoor
shopping
center.
**Change
one letter.**

1. A round object
used in games.
**Change
one letter.**

$\underline{B} \ \underline{i} \ \underline{l} \ \underline{l}$

Partner Poems & Word Ladders for Building Foundational Literacy Skills: K–2 © by Harrison, Rasinski & Fresch, Scholastic Teaching Solutions

Name _____

Read the clues. Then, write the words.
Start at the bottom and climb to the top.

Where the Wind Blows

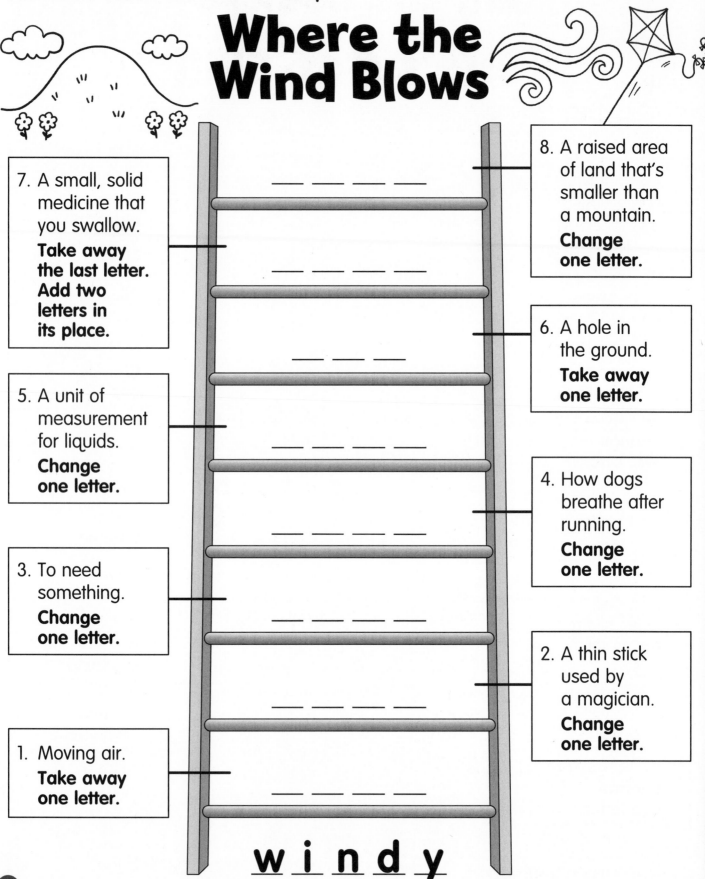

7. A small, solid medicine that you swallow.
Take away the last letter. Add two letters in its place.

5. A unit of measurement for liquids.
Change one letter.

3. To need something.
Change one letter.

1. Moving air.
Take away one letter.

8. A raised area of land that's smaller than a mountain.
Change one letter.

6. A hole in the ground.
Take away one letter.

4. How dogs breathe after running.
Change one letter.

2. A thin stick used by a magician.
Change one letter.

— — — — —

— — — — —

— — — —

— — — —

— — — —

— — — —

— — — —

w i n d y

Fill the Bucket

Objective: Children will suggest other *-ill* words not found in the poem.

Materials

- "Our Hero Jill" (page 54)
- a bucket (or any small container)
- slips of paper for writing individual words
- pencils

Procedure

1. Invite the class to read the poem aloud. Have children take turns reading 1st Voice and 2nd Voice.

2. Distribute slips of paper and pencils to children. Have them write each of the 12 *-ill* words found in the poem on a slip of paper. (*hill, Jill, Bill, shrill, chill, grill, fill, dill, still, skill, ill, pill*)

3. Provide additional slips of paper. Ask children to work with a partner to write any other words they know that contain *-ill*. (See list at right.)

4. Collect the slips of paper and place them facedown on a table.

5. Invite children to take turns picking a slip of paper and reading aloud the word on it. If a child reads the word correctly, he or she can throw the slip of paper in the bucket. Allow children to ask a buddy for help reading a word, if needed.

-ill words		
bill	**chill**	bazillion
Bill	drill	billion
dill	frill	illness
fill	**grill**	gorilla
gill	krill	million
hill	quill	pillage
ill	**shrill**	trillion
Jill	**skill**	village
mill	spill	zillion
pill	**still**	
sill	swill	
will	thrill	
	twill	

Assessment: Circulate as children come up with their own *-ill* words. Who is able to think of more words? How well do children read aloud each word to "fill the bucket?" Create small groups to provide additional practice reading the words.

Wondering about *Phil*?

Many times, names do not match easily with phonograms we are examining. In the case of Phil, the name may be the nickname for Phillip, which contains the phonogram *-ill*. By the way, see if children notice that Bill is a nickname for William and that both names have the *-ill* phonogram!

Dim, Grim Jim

1st Voice	All Together	2nd Voice

1st Voice

Jim was sad.
His mood was bad.
Things looked dim
for grim old Jim.

All Together

**Poor old sad, bad,
dim, grim Jim.**

2nd Voice

*Across the road
lived Kim and Tim.
Kim was prim,
and Tim was slim.
They both were friends
of grim old Jim.*

**Poor old sad, bad,
dim, grim Jim.**

*Prim Kim told
her brother Tim,
"Let's go cheer up
grim old Jim."*

**Poor old sad, bad,
dim, grim Jim.**

(continued)

1st Voice **All Together** **2nd Voice**

"Go away,"
Jim said to Kim.
"What do you want?"
he said to Tim.

"To cheer you up,"
Kim said to Jim.
"Jim," said Tim
on a sudden whim,
"we came to take you
for a swim."

"Swim?" said Jim
to Kim and Tim.
"Swim," said Tim
and Kim to Jim.

**And swimming did
the trick for him.
No more sad, bad,
dim, grim Jim!**

Name _____

Read the clues. Then, write the words.
Start at the bottom and climb to the top.

Lighten Up!

7. Gloomy; another word to describe Jim. **Change one letter.**

6. To make neat by cutting off little bits. **Change one letter.**

5. A journey. Also, to stumble and fall. **Add one letter.**

4. A useful hint. Also, extra money given to a worker for good service. **Change one letter.**

3. The reddish part that surrounds the mouth. **Take away one letter.**

2. What might happen if you step on a banana peel. **Change one letter.**

1. Thin or small in build. **Take away the first letter. Add two letters in its place.**

d i m

Name _____

Read the clues. Then, write the words.
Start at the bottom and climb to the top.

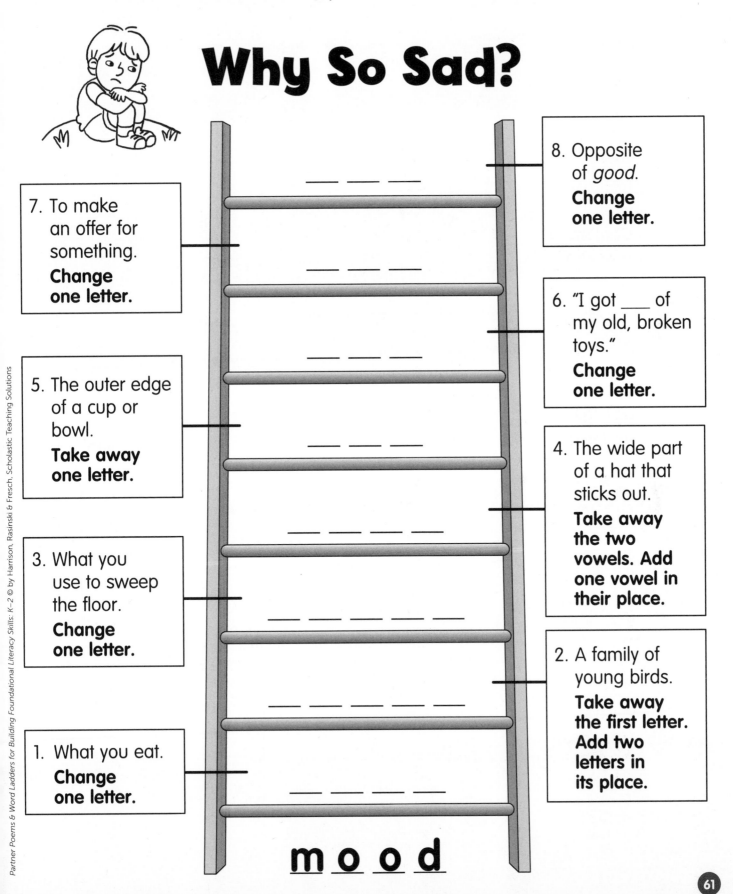

Why So Sad?

8. Opposite of *good*.
Change one letter.

7. To make an offer for something.
Change one letter.

6. "I got ___ of my old, broken toys."
Change one letter.

5. The outer edge of a cup or bowl.
Take away one letter.

4. The wide part of a hat that sticks out.
Take away the two vowels. Add one vowel in their place.

3. What you use to sweep the floor.
Change one letter.

2. A family of young birds.
Take away the first letter. Add two letters in its place.

1. What you eat.
Change one letter.

m o o d

Partner Poems & Word Ladders for Building Foundational Literacy Skills: K–2 © by Harrison, Rasinski & Fresch, Scholastic Teaching Solutions

Retelling a Story

Objective: Children will create a narrative story using the poem as a model.

Materials

- "Dim, Grim Jim" (page 58)
- writing paper

-im words		
dim	brim	chimney
him	**grim**	chimp
Jim	**prim**	immune
Kim	shim	impact
rim	skim	impede
Tim	**slim**	limit
vim	**swim**	shimmy
	trim	simmer
	whim	

Procedure

1. Invite children to read the poem aloud. You can have individual children or partners read the 1st Voice and 2nd Voice, while the rest of the class reads the All Together voice. Invite several children to take turns reading the 1st and 2nd Voices to provide practice in fluency and to understand the "story" in the poem.

2. Share the following incomplete short story to children (created from the poem).

> Once there was a _____ man named _____. He was always in a _____ mood. _____ and _____ lived across the road from _____. One day _____ suggested they cheer up _____. So they invited him to _____. _____'s mood changed! He was no longer _____, _____, _____, or _____!

3. Ask children to help fill in the blanks. Allow them to refer back to the poem, if necessary.

4. Pair up children. Have partners work together and use the last three sentences to write their own adventure to improve the man's mood.

> So they invited him to _____. _____'s mood changed! He was _____!

5. Encourage children to share their stories by reading them aloud.

Assessment: Track which children can assist in filling in the blanks. Are there any children who cannot help? They may need additional opportunities to read the poem to understand the story. Observe the adventures written by the student partners. This is a great formative assessment opportunity as they attempt new vocabulary and spellings.

Identical Twins?

1st Voice

You and Jill dress alike.

I see you have the same eyes,

I see she has some scratches
on her chin and shin.

Your feet are large,
hers are small.

You're sort of wide,
Jill is thin.

Her hair is curly,
yours is straight.

It's hard to know
how to tell you from your twin.

2nd Voice

She's my twin.

the same grin.

She took a spill,
and it was hard on Jill's skin.

She's sort of short,
I'm rather tall.

It's just the light
I'm standing in.

I'm sixteen,
Jill is eight.

If you guess that I'm not Jill,
you win!

Name _____

Read the clues. Then, write the words.
Start at the bottom and climb to the top.

Seeing Double

7. The name of one of the twins in the poem.
Change one letter.

5. "Mom asked me to ___ the bucket with water."
Change one letter.

3. A machine that blows air for cooling.
Change one letter.

1. Opposite of *lose*.
Take away one letter.

6. What a fish uses for breathing.
Change one letter.

4. The season that comes after summer.
Take away one letter. Add two letters in its place.

2. Part of a fish's body that's used for moving.
Change one letter.

__ __ __ __

__ __ __ __

__ __ __ __

__ __ __ __

__ __ __ __

__ __ __ __

t w i n

Partner Poems & Word Ladders for Building Foundational Literacy Skills: K–2 © by Harrison, Rasinski & Fresch, Scholastic Teaching Solutions

Name _____

Read the clues. Then, write the words.
Start at the bottom and climb to the top.

Can't Win

7. A bad smell or odor.
Change two letters.

5. The ability to do something very well.
Take away one letter. Add two letters in its place.

3. This covers your whole body.
Change one letter.

1. To whirl around, like a top.
Add one letter to the beginning.

8. Type of metal often used in cans.
Take away two letters.

6. To be quiet; not moving.
Change one letter.

4. Low-fat milk.
Change one letter.

2. The front part of your leg between the knee and ankle.
Change one letter.

_ _ _ _

_ _ _ _ _

_ _ _ _ _

_ _ _ _ _

_ _ _ _ _

_ _ _ _

_ _ _ _

p i n

Partner Poems & Word Ladders for Building Foundational Literacy Skills: K–2 © by Harrison, Rasinski & Fresch, Scholastic Teaching Solutions

Word Dominoes

Objective: Children will create and play dominoes, using *-in* words.

Materials

- "Identical Twins?" (page 63)
- chart paper
- 3-by-5-inch index cards (Cut each card into three 3-inch strips. You'll need at least four strips for each child.)
- pencils

Procedure

1. Invite the class to read the poem aloud. Have children take turns reading 1st Voice and 2nd Voice. After several readings, ask children to find and highlight the *-in* words in the poem.

2. Next, ask children to think of other *-in* words not used in the poem. List them on chart paper. Use the list at right to assist you in giving clues to new words (for example, *A top is fun to ___*).

-in words		
bin	**chin**	begin
din	**grin**	cousin
in	**shin**	induce
kin	**skin**	inset
pin	spin	into
sin	**thin**	login
tin	**twin**	origin
win		satin

3. To make word dominoes, give each child four card strips. Read aloud an *-in* word and ask children to write it on the bottom of a card strip. Read aloud three more *-in* words for them to write on the remaining cards.

4. Have children shuffle around their card strips. (This way, everyone's dominoes are slightly different.) Then have them turn their cards so the words they wrote are now upside-down. Read aloud four more *-in* words for children to write on the bottom of their cards.

5. Divide the class into small groups and show children how to play Word Dominoes: First, combine the players' cards and shuffle them together. Then, deal the cards to the players. The first player reads aloud a word and lays the card with that word on the table. The next player must match the same word end-to-end. If the player does not have a matching word, he or she loses a turn. Play continues until children use all their cards or can no longer make matches.

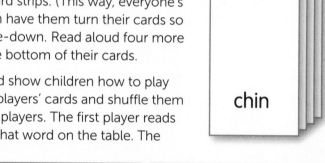

6. To extend the game, create more word dominoes with other words from the list.

Assessment: Check that children correctly spell the words as they create their dominoes. Listen as they play the game to see if they correctly read the words.

If I Were the King

| 1st Voice | All Together | 2nd Voice |

1st Voice

What would you do
if you were the king?

If you were the king.

2nd Voice

If I were the king?

*Each morning
a thousand
birds on the wing
would sing me awake,
if I were the king.*

All Together

**What about you?
What would you do?**

1st Voice

If I were the king,
bees wouldn't sting.
Night and day
I'd hear the ding
of ice cream trucks,
if I were the king.

All Together

**What about you?
What would you do?**

(continued)

1st Voice	**All Together**	**2nd Voice**
		If I were the king,
		I would swing all day
		in my royal swing.
		I'd wear a gumdrop
		for my royal ring,
		if I were the king.
	What about you?	
	What would you do?	
If I were the king,		
here's what I'd do.		
I'd choose a friend		
exactly like you.		
		I'd choose a friend
		like you for me,
		a friend who makes
		my heart sing.
Lucky me,		
lucky you.		
		Lucky us.
It's true!		
		It's true!
	What about you?	
	What would you do?	
	What one special thing,	
	if you were the king?	

Name _____

Read the clues. Then, write the words.
Start at the bottom and climb to the top.

King for a Day

7. The season after winter.
Change one letter.

6. A thin rope or thread.
Add one letter.

5. An angry bee might do this.
Add one letter.

4. What you do with a song.
Take away one letter.

3. Playground equipment.
Add one letter to the beginning.

2. A body part of a bird.
Change one letter.

1. Jewelry worn on a finger.
Change one letter.

k i n g

69

Name _____

Read the clues. Then, write the words.
Start at the bottom and climb to the top.

Best Friends

8. What a good friend can make your heart do.
Take away one letter.

7. A loop of cloth used to support a broken arm.
Change one letter.

6. To move something back and forth.
Add a letter to the beginning and the end.

5. Opposite of *lose*.
Change one letter.

4. To attach a picture to a bulletin board, for example.
Change one letter.

3. Something you use to write with ink.
Change one letter.

2. A fox's home. Also, a cozy room where you might play.
Move the letters around.

1. Opposite of *beginning*.
Take away three letters.

f r i e n d

Partner Poems & Word Ladders for Building Foundational Literacy Skills: K–2 © by Harrison, Rasinski & Fresch, Scholastic Teaching Solutions

If...Then Statements

Objective: Children will write hypothesis/conclusion ("if . . . then") statements about the poem. Children will create their own hypothesis/conclusion statements similar to those in the poem.

Materials
- "If I Were the King" (page 67)
- writing paper

Procedure

1. Invite children to read the poem aloud. Have pairs of children read 1st Voice and 2nd Voice, while the rest of the class reads the All Together voice.

2. Discuss what each person (voice) in the poem would have or do if he were king. *(A thousand birds on the wing would sing him awake; bees wouldn't sting; he would hear the ding of the ice cream truck night and day; he would swing all day in the royal swing; he would wear a gumdrop for a ring; he would have you for a friend)*

-ing words		
bing	bling	dingo
ding	bring	jingle
king	cling	kingdom
ping	fling	kingly
ring	sling	**morning**
sing	**sting**	single
ting	**swing**	tingle
wing	**thing**	
zing		

3. On whiteboard or other display chart, write the following sentence prompt six times:

    If I were the king, then _____.

    Invite children to help you complete each sentence based on the poem and your discussion of what the king would have or do.

4. Distribute writing paper to children, and have them write the same sentence prompt on their paper:

    If I were the king, then _____.

    Ask children to complete the sentence with what they would want to do or have if they were king. Encourage them to share their if/then statements with the class.

Assessment: Observe which children contribute to the conversation. Consider how children finished their if/then statements. Have children share their statements with the class or a small group. Do they understand the "if . . . then" idea?

Shrinking Marbles

1st Voice	All Together	2nd Voice
I got my marbles muddy and they began to stink.		
	Ugh ack yuck ick	
		They began to stink.
I had to clean my marbles, so I began to think.		
	What to do? What to do?	
		He began to think.
I heated soapy water and dropped them in the sink.		
	Ow ow hot hot	
		He dropped them in the sink.

(continued)

Partner Poems & Word Ladders for Building Foundational Literacy Skills: K–2 © by Harrison, Rasinski & Fresch, Scholastic Teaching Solutions

1st Voice	**All Together**	**2nd Voice**
I scrubbed my muddy marbles till I could hear them clink.		
	Clink plink clink tink	
		He could hear them clink.
My water was so soapy it turned my marbles pink.		
	Ick yuck ack ugh	
		He turned his marbles pink.
That heated soapy water made my marbles shrink.		
	Ow ow hot hot	
		It made his marbles shrink.
Now when I play marbles, I need a tiny rink.		
	Teeny-tiny marbles	
		need a teeny-tiny rink.

Partner Poems & Word Ladders for Building Foundational Literacy Skills: K–2 © by Harrison, Rasinski & Fresch, Scholastic Teaching Solutions

Name _____

Read the clues. Then, write the words.
Start at the bottom and climb to the top.

Eye See You

7. To close one eye quickly. **Change one letter.**

_ _ _ _ _

6. A light reddish color. **Take away two letters. Add one letter in their place.**

5. What you do with your brain. **Change one letter.**

_ _ _ _ _

4. To tell someone you are grateful. "Be sure to ___ your friend for the gift." **Add one letter.**

3. A large container for holding liquids, like water. **Change one letter.**

_ _ _ _ _

2. A place where you put money for saving. **Take away one letter.**

1. Paper that has nothing written on it. **Change one letter.**

_ _ _ _ _ _

b l i n k

Partner Poems & Word Ladders for Building Foundational Literacy Skills: K–2 © by Harrison, Rasinski & Fresch, Scholastic Teaching Solutions

Name _____

Read the clues. Then, write the words.
Start at the bottom and climb to the top.

Thirsty?

8. A white liquid that children like to drink.
Change one letter.

7. A small animal with dark, silky fur.
Change one letter.

6. Opposite of *float*. Also, where you might wash dishes.
Change one letter.

5. What you do with a song.
Take away one letter.

4. What an angry bee might do.
Change one letter.

3. An unpleasant odor or smell.
Take away "hr." Add one letter in their place.

2. To make something smaller.
Add two letters to the beginning.

1. A smooth surface used for ice skating. Also, a playing area for marbles in the story.
Take away one letter.

— — — — —

— — — —

— — — —

— — — —

— — — — —

— — — — —

— — — — — —

— — — —

d r i n k

Partner Poems & Word Ladders for Building Foundational Literacy Skills: K–2 © by Harrison, Rasinski & Fresch, Scholastic Teaching Solutions

75

Link the Phonogram

Objective: Children will link single consonants and consonant blends to the phonogram -ink to create real words.

Materials

- "Shrinking Marbles" (page 72)
- Consonant Letter and Cluster Cards, cut into strips (pages 125–127)
- -ink phonogram printed on a card (for each child or pair of children)

Procedure

1. Invite children to read the poem aloud. Ask them to find the -ink words in the poem.

2. You can have children work independently or in pairs. Give each child or pair consonant strips (letters or blends, depending on ability) and the -ink phonogram card.

3. Have children slide the -ink card along the consonant strips, pausing at each letter or blend. Ask them to blend the sounds and then share what word it makes. Alternatively, you can have them write the word on a separate sheet of paper.

4. If combining a letter or blend with -ink does not make a real word, tell children to cross that consonant off the strip.

Assessment: Observe children as they blend across the word. Do they create real words? Does any child need additional practice blending across the sounds? Revisit this activity in small groups with children who need more support.

g	bl	-ink
m	cr	
t	fr	
z	pl	
	sk	

-ink words		
dink	blink	crinkle
ink	brink	periwinkle
kink	**clink**	rethink
link	drink	sprinkle
mink	**plink**	tinker
pink	**shrink**	twinkle
rink	skink	unlink
sink	slink	winkle
tink	**stink**	wrinkle
wink	**think**	

But Can He Sip?

1st Voice

My dog can skip.

Flip? My dog
can skip and flip.

Rip? Of course
my dog can rip.
My dog can skip
and flip and rip.

My dog can yip!

2nd Voice

Big deal.
Your dog can skip.
But can he flip?

But can he rip?

Good. Fine.
Your dog can rip.
I wonder, though,
can he yip?

But can he zip?

(continued)

Partner Poems & Word Ladders for Building Foundational Literacy Skills: K–2 © by Harrison, Rasinski & Fresch, Scholastic Teaching Solutions

1st Voice

My dog can zip!

My dog
can skip
and flip
and rip
and yip
and zip
and sip.

2nd Voice

But can he sip?

Your dog
can skip

and rip

and zip

It seems to me
your dog is hip!

and flip

and yip

and sip.

Name _____

**Read the clues. Then, write the words.
Start at the bottom and climb to the top.**

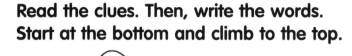

Way to Go

8. A word that describes the dog in the story. Also, a body part. **Take away one letter.**

7. A large boat. **Change one letter.**

6. What might happen if you walk on ice. **Change one letter.**

5. To cut something off with scissors. **Change one letter.**

4. You ___ at the end of a play to show how much you enjoyed it. **Add one letter.**

3. When you sit, the part of your body between the knees and hips. **Take away one letter.**

2. What birds do with their wings to fly. **Change one letter.**

1. To toss in the air, like a coin. **Add one letter to the beginning.**

l i p

Name _____

Read the clues. Then, write the words.
Start at the bottom and climb to the top.

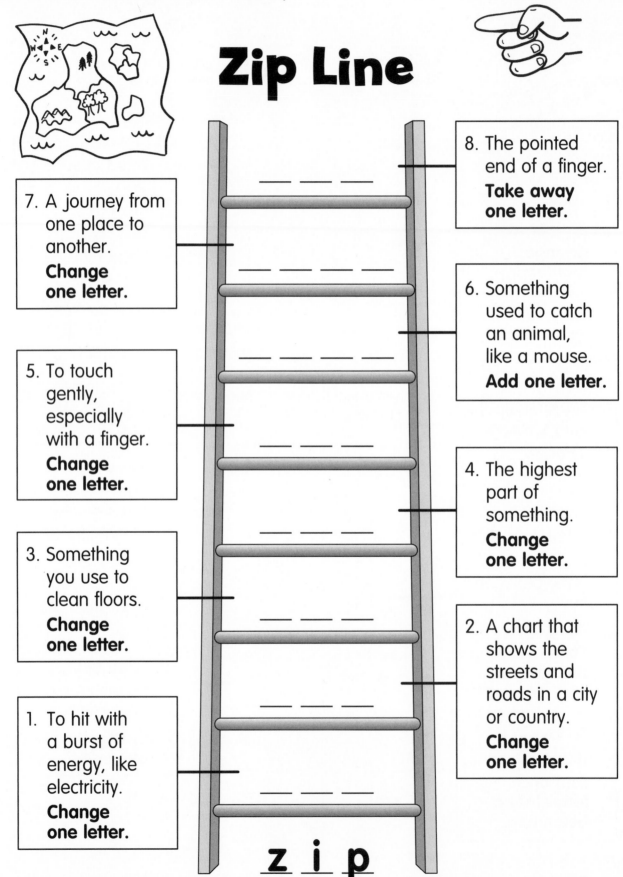

Zip Line

8. The pointed end of a finger. **Take away one letter.**

7. A journey from one place to another. **Change one letter.**

6. Something used to catch an animal, like a mouse. **Add one letter.**

5. To touch gently, especially with a finger. **Change one letter.**

4. The highest part of something. **Change one letter.**

3. Something you use to clean floors. **Change one letter.**

2. A chart that shows the streets and roads in a city or country. **Change one letter.**

1. To hit with a burst of energy, like electricity. **Change one letter.**

z i p

Partner Poems & Word Ladders for Building Foundational Literacy Skills: K–2 © by Harrison, Rasinski & Fresch, Scholastic Teaching Solutions

Flip Book

Objective: Children will create a flip book using -*ip* words.

Materials

- "But Can He Sip?" (page 77)
- index card per child
- 8 half index cards per child
- pencils
- stapler

Procedure

1. Invite the class to read the poem aloud, giving several children a turn at reading 1st Voice and 2nd Voice. Ask children to find the -*ip* words in the poem.

2. Give each child an index card. Have children draw a line down the middle of the index card and write "-*ip*" in the box on the right.

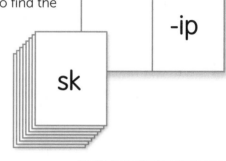

3. Give each child eight half index cards. Ask children to review the -*ip* words in the poem. Then, have them pick four consonants or consonant blends to write on each of four half index cards to make -*ip* words they see in the poem.

4. Next, ask them to write the following blends, one on each of the remaining four half index cards: *gr, sn, str, tr*. (Alternatively, you can ask them to think of -*ip* words they know and write the consonant or consonant blend needed to make the word.)

5. Staple all eight half index cards on top of the full-size card that has -*ip* on the right-hand side.

6. Ask children to read the word on the top card, then flip to the next half index card to see a new beginning sound. Have them take turns reading aloud a word from their flip book. You can provide other blends or you can leave blank cards for children to come up with their own -*ip* words to add to their flip books.

Assessment: Do children correctly blend across the beginning sound(s) and -*ip*? Do they need guidance on how to sound across to blend the sounds?

-*ip* words		
dip	blip	catnip
hip	chip	diplomat
lip	clip	equip
nip	drip	gossip
pip	**flip**	nonslip
rip	grip	parsnip
sip	quip	slippery
tip	ship	tulip
yip	**skip**	unzip
zip	slip	worship
	snip	yippee
	strip	zipper
	trip	
	whip	

A Hissy Fit

1st Voice

My lizard threw
a hissy fit.

I think he swallowed
a cherry pit.

At first, I thought,
"It's just a snit."
But no, it was
a hissy fit.
He switched his tail
like he could spit.
His tongue flew out . . .

I told him, "Cool it.
Settle. Sit."

Not one bit.

Yes. That's it.
I'm done. I quit.

2nd Voice

Why did he throw
a hissy fit?

Man, that took
a lot of grit.

That little twit!

And did he quit?

He threw another
hissy fit?

I like your lizard,
but not his fit.

Name _____

Read the clues. Then, write the words.
Start at the bottom and climb to the top.

What Is It?

7. To strike something, as with a baseball bat. **Change one letter.**

_ _ _ _

6. A covering for the head. **Change one letter.**

5. To tap something lightly or gently. **Change one letter.**

_ _ _ _

4. A hole in the ground. **Take away two letters.**

_ _ _ _

3. To divide something. **Add one letter in the middle.**

_ _ _ _ _

2. To force saliva out of your mouth. **Change one letter.**

_ _ _ _ _

1. A short play or act. **Change two letters.**

_ _ _ _

q u i t

Partner Poems & Word Ladders for Building Foundational Literacy Skills: K–2 © by Harrison, Rasinski & Fresch, Scholastic Teaching Solutions

Name _____

Read the clues. Then, write the words.
Start at the bottom and climb to the top.

Nice Lizard

8. Healthy and strong. Also, a bad mood, like what the lizard threw in the story. **Change one letter.**

7. What you do in a chair. **Take away one letter.**

6. A short play or act. **Change the two letters in the middle.**

5. To leave quickly. Also, something you might say to a cat. **Change one letter.**

4. A mark left on the skin after a wound has healed. **Add one letter to the beginning.**

3. An automobile. **Take away one letter.**

2. A stiff paper. Also, what you might send someone on their birthday. **Change one letter.**

1. Opposite of *soft*. **Take away the first three letters. Add one letter in their place.**

l i z a r d

Partner Poems & Word Ladders for Building Foundational Literacy Skills: K–2 © by Harrison, Rasinski & Fresch, Scholastic Teaching Solutions

Mix It Up! Pass It On!

Objective: Children will scramble and unscramble letters of *-it* words from the poem.

Materials

- "A Hissy Fit" (page 82)
- highlighters
- lined paper
- pencils

Procedure

1. Have children read the poem aloud several times, giving different pairs the opportunity to read 1st Voice and 2nd Voice.

2. Ask children: *What phonogram do you hear most often?* (-it) Ask them to help you highlight these words on the poem. (Or you can have individual copies for children to highlight on their own or with a partner.)

3. Give children lined paper, asking them to number the lines from 1 to 5. (You can increase the number to 8, depending on time and readiness of the children.)

-it words		
bit	flit	audit
fit	**grit**	biscuit
hit	knit	digit
it	**quit**	habit
kit	skit	inherit
lit	slit	legit
nit	**snit**	omit
pit	**spit**	remit
sit	split	visit
wit	sprit	vomit
zit	**twit**	witness

4. Tell children to choose one of the highlighted words in the poem and mix up the letters as they write it on line 1. For example, write *ti* for the word *it* from the poem. Have them repeat for five words, scrambling the letters for each word.

5. After children have completed their list, tell them to pass the paper to a neighbor. That child must unscramble the letters to make the word from the poem and then pass the paper again to the next person. Continue until all the words on each paper have been unscrambled.

6. Write the following on the board or on chart paper: *kist, thi, ipt, stil.* Bring children together and ask if anyone can unscramble the letters to make real words. Remind them each word must have *-it* in it, guiding them to look at the remaining letters to figure out the word.

Assessment: Are the children able to unscramble the words? Watch as they work on these to see if they use the print as reference for correct spelling. Use the time during step 6 to target children who need additional support.

Rob and Bob

1st Voice

In a tiny town called Gobble Knob,
there lived a man named Rob.

Rob was proud of how he looked,
his house, his clothes, his job.

Rob the snob from Gobble Knob
looked down his nose at Bob,

When Rob the snob lost his job,
you should have heard him sob.
He lost his house and fancy clothes
and soon looked much like Bob.

Rob was never again a snob.
Today in Gobble Knob,

2nd Voice

Across the town, across the field,
lived poor old raggedy Bob.

Rob thought Bob looked like a slob
and rougher than a cob.

while Bob the slob from Gobble Knob
was always kind to Rob.

That's when poor old raggedy Bob
held out a hand to Rob,
loaned him clothes, shared his food,
and gave new hope to Rob.

they say there are no better friends
than raggedy Rob and Bob.

Name _____

Read the clues. Then, write the words.
Start at the bottom and climb to the top.

Buddies

7. The old raggedy character from the story.
Change one letter.

___ ___ ___

6. To gently throw a ball in the air.
Change one letter.

___ ___ ___

5. To breathe in short gasps from crying hard.
Change one letter.

___ ___ ___

4. Corn on the ___.
Change one letter.

___ ___ ___

3. A taxi.
Change one letter.

___ ___ ___

2. A quick punch.
Change one letter.

___ ___ ___

1. Work that is done for pay.
Change one letter.

___ ___ ___

R o b

Read the clues. Then, write the words.
Start at the bottom and climb to the top.

Don't Look Down

7. A flower. Also, a pinkish color.
Take away one letter. Add two letters in its place.

_ _ _ _ _

8. Snobby Rob looked down his ___ at raggedy old Bob.
Change one letter.

_ _ _ _

5. To move up and down on water. Also, short for Robert.
Change one letter.

_ _ _ _

6. To steal from someone.
Change one letter.

_ _ _

3. A person's forehead.
Take away one letter.

_ _ _

4. The front of a ship. Also, what you use to shoot arrows.
Take away one letter.

_ _ _ _ _

1. To bring your eyebrows together to show anger.
Take away one letter. Add two letters in its place.

_ _ _ _ _

2. A dark color, like on bears and chocolate.
Change one letter.

_ _ _ _

d o w n

Synonyms

Objective: Children will select words from the poem and suggest possible synonyms.

Materials

- "Rob and Bob" (page 86)
- highlighters

Procedure

1. Provide print copies of the poem for pairs of children. Have children read the poem several times, giving different pairs the opportunity to read 1st Voice and 2nd Voice.

2. Ask pairs of children to look over their copy of the poem and highlight some words for which they could substitute a synonym (word or phrase). For example, highlight *man* and above it, write one (or all) of the following: *fellow, guy, gentleman*.

-*ob* words		
Bob	blob	bobsled
cob	glob	cobbler
gob	**knob**	**gobble**
job	**slob**	goblet
lob	**snob**	hobby
mob	throb	kebob
Rob		object
sob		obtain

3. Give children time to work through the poem. Here are other suggestions: *town*—city, village; *slob*—messy person, slacker; *snob*—show-off, bragger; *kind*—thoughtful, nice; *sob*—cry, weep; *loaned*—gave, shared; *friends*—buddies, pals.

4. Invite children to share their synonyms. Choose some child-suggested synonyms to replace words in the poem, then have children read aloud the new version. (For instance: *In a small village named Gobble Knob, there resided a gentleman called Rob.*)

Assessment: Do children tap into their vocabulary knowledge to suggest synonyms? Listen as they talk about possibilities as this may indicate their need for more vocabulary experiences.

Stop! Stop!

1st Voice	2nd Voice	3rd Voice

1st Voice

raindrop

shop shop
thirsty

slop slop
rained on

stop stop!

2nd Voice

plop plop
rooftop

mop mop
rain boots

crop crop
mud puddle

hop hop
pigpen

sop sop
want to play

stop stop!

3rd Voice

drop drop
wet floor

glop glop
garump garump

stop stop!

Name _____

Read the clues. Then, write the words.
Start at the bottom and climb to the top.

STOP

It's Raining!

8. A bead of rain.
Change
two letters.

7. To end
an activity.
Add one
letter to the
beginning.

6. Opposite
of *bottom*.
Change
one letter.

5. To strike lightly,
as with a
finger.
Change
one letter.

4. A short period
of sleep.
Change
one letter.

3. A small bite,
like from
a puppy.
Move the
letters around.

2. To hold
something
firmly in place.
Take away
one letter.

1. Feeling of hurt,
like from a cut.
Change
one letter.

— — — —

— — — —

— — — —

— — — —

— — — —

— — — —

— — — —

r a i n

Name _____

Read the clues. Then, write the words.
Start at the bottom and climb to the top.

On the Farm

8. A tool for writing with ink. Also, a small, closed area for farm animals.
Change one letter.

7. A female bird you might find on a farm.
Change one letter.

6. Something Mom might call you; short for *honey*.
Change one letter.

5. To jump on one foot.
Change one letter.

4. The highest part of something.
Change one letter.

3. A heavy weight; 2,000 pounds.
Change one letter.

2. A metal used to make cans.
Change one letter.

1. A small, pointed piece of metal used to fasten or attach things.
Change one letter.

p i g

Words Battleship

Objective: Children will write -op words into a grid, then play Words Battleship with a partner.

Materials

- "Stop! Stop!" (page 90)
- 2 blank labeled grids for each child (see right)
- lined paper
- pencils
- file folders (or other dividers for privacy)

Procedure

1. Have children read the poem aloud several times, giving different pairs the opportunity to read 1st, 2nd, or 3rd Voice.

2. Distribute lined paper to children. Ask them to find 12 -op words in the poem and write them on their paper.

3. Give each child one blank grid and a file folder. Explain that you will read aloud an -op word from the poem and children should write it in any square on their grid. Have them open the file folder to keep anyone from seeing where they write each word. (They will have four unused boxes.)

4. Next, pair up children. Have partners sit across from each other, using their folders to keep their grids hidden. Give each child an extra blank grid. Explain to children how to read the coordinate of each box—first by looking at the letters across the top row, then looking at the numbers in the first column.

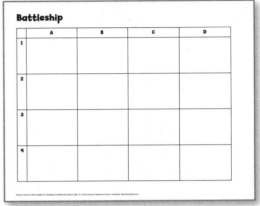

(Available online.)

-op words		
bop	chop	adopt
cop	**crop**	atop
hop	**drop**	copy
lop	flop	laptop
mop	**glop**	lollipop
pop	**plop**	option
sop	prop	opera
top	**shop**	**raindrop**
	slop	**rooftop**
	stop	tiptop

5. You may want to model how to play Words Battleship. First, show how you write words in the squares on your grid. Then, call on a child to give you a coordinate (for example, A-2) and then show the class how you look up that coordinate in your grid. Next, say "Hit" or "Miss," depending on whether there is a word in that box. Show how you keep track of their guesses on a blank grid by writing an X on the coordinate.

6. To play, players take turns saying a coordinate, such as A-1. Remind them to X this coordinate on their blank grid to keep track of their guesses. If the partner has a word in that box, he must say "Hit," read the word aloud, and cross it off his grid. If there is no word, he says "Miss." Players continue taking turns until one partner's words have all been "hit."

Assessment: Check to see if children correctly spell the words as they write them in the grid. Observe as children read aloud their "Hit" word.

Little Scott

1st Voice

The day was bright,
the sun was hot.

2nd Voice

A perfect day
to play a lot.

Till Mama said,
"Take care of Scott."

Your baby brother?
Little Scott?

Little Scott,
the little snot.

On the spot
your day was shot.

Just because
she had to shop.

Your play day
went down the pot.

I hosed a spot
of muddy glop
and set him in it
—ha!—kerplop.

Grounded

I bet he was
a happy tot.

Till Mom came home . . .
and she was not.

You got in trouble
over Scott?

I'm grounded now
until I rot.

Partner Poems & Word Ladders for Building Foundational Literacy Skills: K–2 © by Harrison Rasinski & Fresch Scholastic Teaching Solutions

Name _____

Read the clues. Then, write the words.
Start at the bottom and climb to the top.

Hey, Kid!

8. A young child.
**Change
one letter.**

7. Opposite
of *bottom*.
**Change
one letter.**

6. A police officer.
**Take away
one letter.**

5. What you do
with an ax.
**Change
one letter.**

4. A store. Also,
to buy things
in a store.
**Change
one letter.**

3. Try, as in
"give it your
best ___."
**Add one
letter to the
beginning.**

2. Opposite
of *cold*.
**Change
one letter.**

1. A type of bed
used when
camping.
**Take away
two letters.**

S c o t t

Partner Poems & Word Ladders for Building Foundational Literacy Skills: K–2 © by Harrison, Rasinski & Fresch, Scholastic Teaching Solutions

Name _____

Read the clues. Then, write the words.
Start at the bottom and climb to the top.

Hot Spot

7. "Today is hot. It is much ___ than yesterday."
Change one letter.

6. A person who makes pots is called a ___.
Add three letters to the end.

5. A kitchen item used to boil water.
Take away one letter.

4. A standing piece of wood that's fixed to hold up something, like a sign.
Move the letters around.

3. A small mark or stain. Also, a common name for a dog.
Move the letters around.

2. Opposite of go.
Change one letter.

1. A place where shoppers buy things.
Take away three letters.

s h o p p e r

96

Hop to the Spot

Objective: Children will hop on "spots" with *-ot* words and read them aloud.

Materials

- "Little Scott" (page 94)
- 12 to 14 sturdy, 9-inch, round paper plates
- marker

Procedure

1. Invite children to read the poem several times, taking turns to read the 1st and 2nd Voices.

2. Show children the paper plates. Ask them to find the *-ot* words in the poem so you can write them on the "spots." Ask children if they know any other *-ot* words for the remaining paper plates.

3. Spread the paper plates around the room. Pair up children. Then ask partners to walk to a "spot," hop on it, and read aloud the word written on it. Have partners check each other for accuracy.

-ot words		
cot	blot	allot
dot	clot	botch
got	knot	gotcha
hot	plot	jackpot
jot	**shot**	ocelot
lot	slot	potluck
not	**snot**	robot
pot	**spot**	**Scott**
rot	trot	subplot
sot		sunspot
tot		teapot

Assessment: Listen as children hop onto the paper plates. Are they able to accurately read the *-ot* words? You can repeat this activity and differentiate the words by the columns in the chart above, grouping children to hop on words that meet their skill level.

Every Word Is True

1st Voice	**All Together**	**2nd Voice**
This is not a great big fib.		
		Every word is true.
I saw a duck. His name was Chuck. He wore a cap. He drove a truck.		
		He saw a duck. *He drove a truck.*
	And every word is true.	
Chuck the duck let out a cluck.		
		Not a quack. *It was a cluck.* *On his lap* *he had a map.*
	And every word is true.	
He dropped his map. His truck got stuck.		
		"Yuck!" said Chuck. *"I'm out of luck."*
A woodchuck came. His name was Huck.		
		Huck saw Chuck *stuck in the guck.*
He pulled and tugged him from the muck.		
		Said Chuck, "I am *a lucky duck!"*
	And every word is true.	

Partner Poems & Word Ladders for Building Foundational Literacy Skills: K–2 © by Harrison, Reinecki & Freeh, Scholastic Teaching Solutions

Name _____

Read the clues. Then, write the words.
Start at the bottom and climb to the top.

Don't Muck It Up

7. What trains ride on. **Add one letter.**

5. A large bag. **Change one letter.**

3. What you do with a lollipop. **Change one letter.**

1. Sound made by a chicken. **Change one letter.**

8. What Chuck the duck drove. **Change one letter.**

6. A short, sharp nail with a flat, broad head. **Change one letter.**

4. Not feeling well; ill. **Change one letter.**

2. Good fortune. **Take away one letter.**

C h u c k

Name _____

Read the clues. Then, write the words.
Start at the bottom and climb to the top.

Chuck It!

8. Hard material that comes from trees. Also, when combined with the first word, a small, furry animal. **Change one letter.**

7. Opposite of *bad*. **Change one letter.**

6. A precious metal used in jewelry. **Add two letters to the end.**

5. Opposite of *stop*. **Change one letter.**

4. Every day try to ____ a good deed. **Take away two letters.**

3. A place where ships load or unload their goods. **Change one letter.**

2. A bird that quacks. **Take away two letters. Add one letter in their place.**

1. Our car got ___ on the muddy road. **Change two letters.**

_c_ _h_ _u_ _c_ _k_

Lucky Match

Objective: Children will create cards with *-uck* words and use them to play a memory game.

Materials

- "Every Word Is True" (page 98)
- highlighter
- 24 index cards in 2 different colors (Cut each index card in half.)
- pencils

Procedure

-*uck* words		
buck	**Chuck**	amuck
duck	**cluck**	bucket
guck	pluck	buckle
Huck	shuck	chuckle
luck	snuck	**lucky**
muck	**stuck**	potluck
puck	struck	pucker
suck	**truck**	unstuck
tuck		**woodchuck**
yuck		

1. Have children read the poem several times, inviting different pairs of children to read 1st Voice and 2nd Voice while the rest of the class reads the All Together voice.

2. Ask children to find the *-uck* words in the poem and highlight them.

3. Divide the class in half. Distribute one color of the half index cards to half the class, the other color to the other half of the class. Ask two children from each group to write *duck* on their cards. Each group will have a matching pair of cards with the word *duck* for playing the game.

4. Continue choosing two children in each group to write an *-uck* word from the poem that you read aloud (*luck, muck, Chuck, cluck, stuck, truck, yuck, woodchuck*). Encourage children to look at the poem for help in spelling their words. You can specifically choose the children who can write the more challenging words.

5. Next, create three additional word pairs by asking children: *What word would you have if you put* p *in front of* luck? (pluck) *What about if you put* s *in front of* truck? (struck) *What would you have if you put* y *at the end of* luck? (lucky) Have two children in each group write the new words.

6. Have children in each group shuffle their cards and place all 24 cards facedown on a table or floor. Then have children in each group take turns playing memory.

Assessment: Do children correctly write the poem words? Who is able to assist in thinking of the words for the last three sets?

A Bad Bug Dream

1st Voice

Last night I had a nightmare.
I dreamed I swallowed a bug.

It was red and green and purple
and crawled inside my jug.

Next, in my nightmare,
I poured it in my mug.

I tried not to swallow,
but halfway down it stuck.

In my dream, it tickled.
I thought I might upchuck.

Somehow I spit it out
clear across the rug.

I woke up very happy,
glad it wasn't a slug.

2nd Voice

You swallowed a bug?
What awful luck!

You swallowed that?
Ick! Yuck!

And down it went,
glug, glug?

The bug stuck?
That little thug!

Poor you!
Oh! Ug!

Too bad you took
that bug chug.

Partner Poems & Word Ladders for Building Foundational Literacy Skills: K–2 © by Harrison Rojecki & French Scholastic Teaching Solutions

Name _____

Read the clues. Then, write the words.
Start at the bottom and climb to the top.

Hugs!

7. The bug in the poem crawled into this kind of container.
Take away two letters. Add one letter in its place.

— — — —

6. To drink something quickly.
Add one letter to the beginning.

— — — —

5. To hold someone tight in a loving way.
Change one letter.

— — —

4. A floor mat made of wool or cloth.
Change one letter.

— — —

3. An old cloth used for cleaning.
Change one letter.

— — —

2. A game in which children chase one another.
Change one letter.

— — —

1. To pull. Also, a game in which two teams pull on a rope.
Change one letter.

— — —

<u>b</u> <u>u</u> <u>g</u>

Name _____

Read the clues. Then, write the words.
Start at the bottom and climb to the top.

Drink Up!

8. Another word for a mug.
Change one letter.

7. What scissors do to paper.
Change one letter.

6. A deep track in the ground, made by wheels.
Change one letter.

5. Food that is spoiled will ___.
Take away one letter.

4. To run at a slow pace.
Take away one letter. Add two letters in its place.

3. Opposite of *a little*. A ___.
Change one letter.

2. A part of a tree that has fallen or been chopped down.
Change one letter.

1. To carry something with great effort.
Change one letter.

m u g

Partner Poems & Word Ladders for Building Foundational Literacy Skills: K–2 © by Harrison, Rasinski & Fresch, Scholastic Teaching Solutions

Bug Out!

Objective: Children will differentiate between words that rhyme with *bug* and words that do not.

Materials

- "A Bad Bug Dream" (page 102)
- 15 copies of bug outline (see right)
- flyswatter
- pencil

Procedure

1. On the bug outline, write 15 words from the poem—the eight *-ug* words from the poem plus seven other words that do not contain *-ug*. You might choose the *-uck* words reviewed or any other word from the poem. (Alternatively, you can hand out the blank bugs to children and have them assist you in writing the words as you read each one aloud.)

2. Invite children to read the poem several times, then ask them to find the *-ug* words. Show them the words you wrote on the bug sheets.

3. Give a child the flyswatter. Show two bugs—one with an *-ug* word, one without. Have the child "swat" the word that does not rhyme with *bug*. Continue with the words, mixing the presentation of *-ug* and non *-ug* words until everyone has had a turn.

Assessment: Do children read across the word pair and select the correct one to swat?

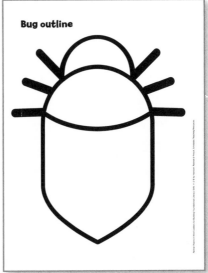

Bug outline

(Available online.)

-ug words		
bug	**chug**	earplug
dug	drug	humbug
hug	**glug**	juggle
jug	plug	ladybug
lug	shrug	rugby
mug	**slug**	rugged
pug	smug	struggle
rug	snug	tugged
tug	**thug**	ugly

Early in the Morning

1st Voice	All Together	2nd Voice

1st Voice

My little brother
plays his drum,

2nd Voice

*rum pum
rum tum tum,*

All Together

early in the morning.

1st Voice

He doesn't stop
to eat or drink.
He hops and pops
till I can't think!

2nd Voice

*rum pum
rum tum tum,*

All Together

early in the morning.

1st Voice

I fear my brain
is turning numb.
I cannot sleep,
I'm feeling glum
from Brother playing
on that drum.

2nd Voice

*rum pum
rum tum tum,*

All Together

early in the morning!

Name _____

**Read the clues. Then, write the words.
Start at the bottom and climb to the top.**

Shhh!

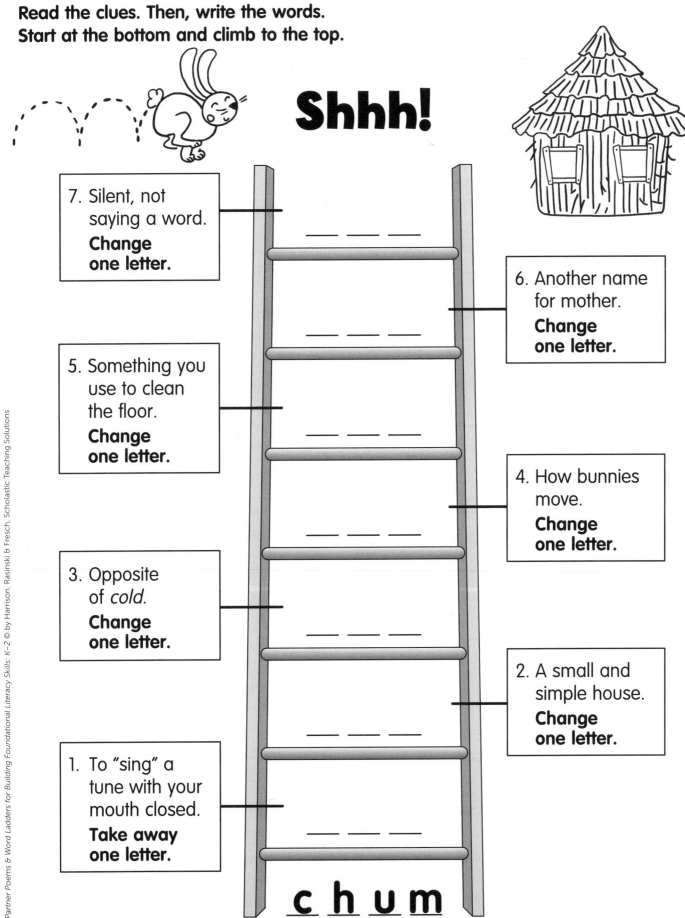

7. Silent, not saying a word. **Change one letter.**

_ _ _ _

6. Another name for mother. **Change one letter.**

_ _ _

5. Something you use to clean the floor. **Change one letter.**

_ _ _ _

4. How bunnies move. **Change one letter.**

_ _ _ _

3. Opposite of *cold*. **Change one letter.**

_ _ _ _

2. A small and simple house. **Change one letter.**

_ _ _ _

1. To "sing" a tune with your mouth closed. **Take away one letter.**

_ _ _ _

c h u m

Name _____

Read the clues. Then, write the words.
Start at the bottom and climb to the top.

On the Beat

7. To play a guitar by brushing fingers on the strings.
Change one letter.

8. The musical instrument the brother in the poem played.
Take away two letters. Add one letter in its place.

6. To walk in a proud way.
Add two letters to the beginning.

5. A deep track in the ground made by a wheel.
Change one letter.

4. To decay or become waste.
Change one letter.

3. Shorter word for *robot*.
Take away one letter.

2. Two things or people.
Take away two letters.

1. To annoy someone.
Take away one letter.

b r o t h e r

Partner Poems & Word Ladders for Building Foundational Literacy Skills: K–2 © by Harrison, Rasinski & Fresch Scholastic Teaching Solutions

Number Circles

Objective: Children will write and identify *-um* words for a game.

Materials

- "Early in the Morning" (page 106)
- highlighter
- chart paper
- Number Circles game board (sheet of paper with 8 large, numbered circles; see right)
- pencils

Procedure

1. Have children take turns reading the poem several times.

2. Point out the word *drum* and ask children if they hear or see any words that rhyme with it. (Accept the word *numb*—see note below that you can share with children.) Highlight the words in the poem and make a list of them on chart paper.

3. Ask children if they can think of any other *-um* words, and add these to your list.

4. Give each child a copy of the Number Circles game board.

5. Choose eight words from your list. (Select the words based on your students' word knowledge, or invite children to help you choose eight words for the game.)

6. To randomize children's game boards, have them count off 1 to 8 (repeating until all children have a number). Tell children to write the first *-um* word you say in the circle that matches the number they called. Then, continue by reading the remaining words one at a time, asking children to choose any blank circle in which to write each word until you've read aloud all eight words from your list.

7. To play, call out an *-um* word from your list. Have children check or cross out that word on their boards. The first child to mark four circles that are next to each other wins. Ask the child who calls four in a row to read aloud their four words. You can continue until more children win.

Assessment: Have children turn in their game boards to check for accuracy in writing the words. Did children correctly spell the words you called? Did the winner correctly read aloud the words? Who might need review of the phonogram?

Wondering about *numb*?

Although *numb* rhymes with the other *-um* words in the poem, it ends with the silent *b*. These words are from long ago, and at one time the /b/ sound was pronounced. Over time English speakers changed the pronunciation of these words to end with the /m/ sound but did not change the spelling. Challenge children to think of words that end in the silent *b* (*lamb, tomb, limb, comb, thumb, crumb, dumb*). Sometimes we hear the /b/ sound in related words (*bombard, crumble, number*).

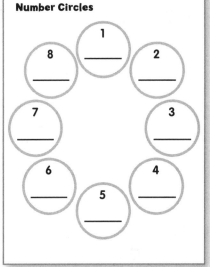

Number Circles

(Available online.)

-um words		
bum	chum	gumbo
gum	**drum**	jumbo
hum	**glum**	lumber
mum	plum	mumble
pum	scum	number
rum	slum	rummy
sum	strum	stumble
tum	thrum	tummy
yum		

Did You Hear That?

1st Voice

Did you hear that?

That bump.

Not really a bump.
More like a whump.

No, not a clump.
More like a whack.

No, I'd say
maybe a clack.

Yes, like that.

Made a thump.
More like a wump.

Whatever it was,
now it's gone.

Carry on.

2nd Voice

What?

No.

Maybe a clump?

Maybe a crack?

Perhaps a smack?

Something jump?

Sounded plump.

What do we do
now that it's gone?

Name _____

Read the clues. Then, write the words.
Start at the bottom and climb to the top.

Make Some Noise

7. A sound in the poem. Also, what you do to open an egg. **Change one letter.**

6. Sound made by a rattle or by striking two things together. **Change one letter.**

5. Sound made by a chicken. **Change two letters.**

4. A group of trees or plants. Also, a sound made by walking heavily. **Add one letter to the beginning.**

3. A bump that might pop up on the body when hit by a ball. **Add one letter to the beginning.**

2. Nickname for an official in a baseball game. **Take away one letter.**

1. The rounded part on the back of a camel. **Take away one letter.**

t h u m p

Partner Poems & Word Ladders for Building Foundational Literacy Skills: K–2 © by Harrison, Rasinski & Fresch, Scholastic Teaching Solutions

Name _____

**Read the clues. Then, write the words.
Start at the bottom and climb to the top.**

In the Wild

8. What's left after a tree has been cut down.
Take away one letter. Add two letters in its place.

7. To knock into something.
Change two letters.

6. A male deer. Also, another word for *one dollar*.
Change one letter.

5. Opposite of *front*.
Change one letter.

4. Not having enough of something.
Change two letters.

3. A kind of light, like for a desk.
Take away one letter.

2. A tool for holding things together.
Change one letter.

1. A group of trees or plants.
Change one letter.

p l u m p

Partner Poems & Word Ladders for Building Foundational Literacy Skills: K–2 © by Harrison, Rasinski & Fresch, Scholastic Teaching Solutions

Web a Word

Objective: Children will web *-ump* words using consonants and consonant blends.

Materials

- "Did You Hear That?" (page 110)
- blank paper
- Consonant Letter and Cluster Cards (pages 125–127)
- scissors
- glue

Procedure

1. Invite children to read the poem several times, giving different pairs opportunity to read 1st Voice and 2nd Voice.

2. Have children find all the *-ump* words in the poem. Ask them what other *-ump* words they know. Write the words on the board where children can see them.

3. Pair up children. Distribute blank paper to each pair. Ask children to write *-ump* at the bottom of the page.

4. Pass out copies of the Consonant Letter and Cluster Cards to each pair. Have them cut apart the consonant cards.

5. With their partner, have children think of *-ump* words. On their paper, have them draw a line from *-ump* and glue a consonant or consonant blend card that, together with *-ump*, would make a word. They may use the poem and the list you created to make as many words as they can. Suggest that they create at least five words.

Assessment: Check that the words created by the partners are correct. Are the children able to create more than five words?

-ump words		
bump	chump	bumper
dump	**clump**	bumpy
hump	grump	crumpet
jump	**plump**	dumpster
lump	slump	grumpy
pump	stump	jumper
rump	**thump**	lumpy
sump	trump	pumpkin
ump	**whump**	rumple
wump		trumpet

Partner Poems & Word Ladders for Building Foundational Literacy Skills: K–2 © by Harrison, Rasinski & Fresch, Scholastic Teaching Solutions

Deep in the Woods

1st Voice	All Together	2nd Voice
The moon was dark,		
		the sun had sunk,
	far off deep in the woods.	
High in a tree, on an acorn bunk,		
		a chipmunk sat, lost in a funk,
and listened to rain,		
		plunk . . . plunk
	far off deep in the woods.	
He sighed, as sad as sad could be,		
		"I have no friend to play with me,
to share some bread and a cup of tea,"		
	far off deep in the woods.	
		Down at the base of the very same trunk
lived a lovely, lonely skunk,		
		who watched the rain in her own skunk funk, plunk . . . plunk . . . plunk
	far off deep in the woods.	

(continued)

1st Voice	**All Together**	**2nd Voice**
"I need a friend," she sadly said,		
		"to share some tea and fresh-baked bread, but all I see is rain instead,"
	far off deep in the woods.	
When morning came, the sun was bright.		
		The end had come to the endless night.
Chipmunk sat on a sunny stump,		
		and there he met the lovely skunk.
To think, they lived in the very same tree!		
		They nodded and talked, and laughed with glee.
He loved her bread,		
		she loved his tea.
Chipmunk and Skunk		
		became best friends,
and that is how		
		their story ends,
	far off deep in the woods.	

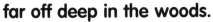

Name _____

Read the clues. Then, write the words.
Start at the bottom and climb to the top.

Lots of Junk

7. A large box in which you might store your junk. **Change two letters.**

   _ _ _ _ _

6. To fool or cheat someone. Also, what you say at Halloween: "___ or treat!" **Add one letter.**

   _ _ _ _ _

5. The clicking sound that a clock or watch makes. **Change one letter.**

   _ _ _ _

4. "Mom will ___ me into bed in ten minutes." **Change one letter.**

   _ _ _ _

3. An animal that says quack. **Change one letter.**

   _ _ _ _

2. To dip a cookie in milk. **Change one letter.**

   _ _ _ _ _

1. Dirty, sticky, or gooey stuff. **Change one letter.**

   _ _ _ _

j u n k

Partner Poems & Word Ladders for Building Foundational Literacy Skills: K–2 © by Harrison, Rasinski & Fresch, Scholastic Teaching Solutions

WORD LADDER 2
-unk

Read the clues. Then, write the words.
Start at the bottom and climb to the top.

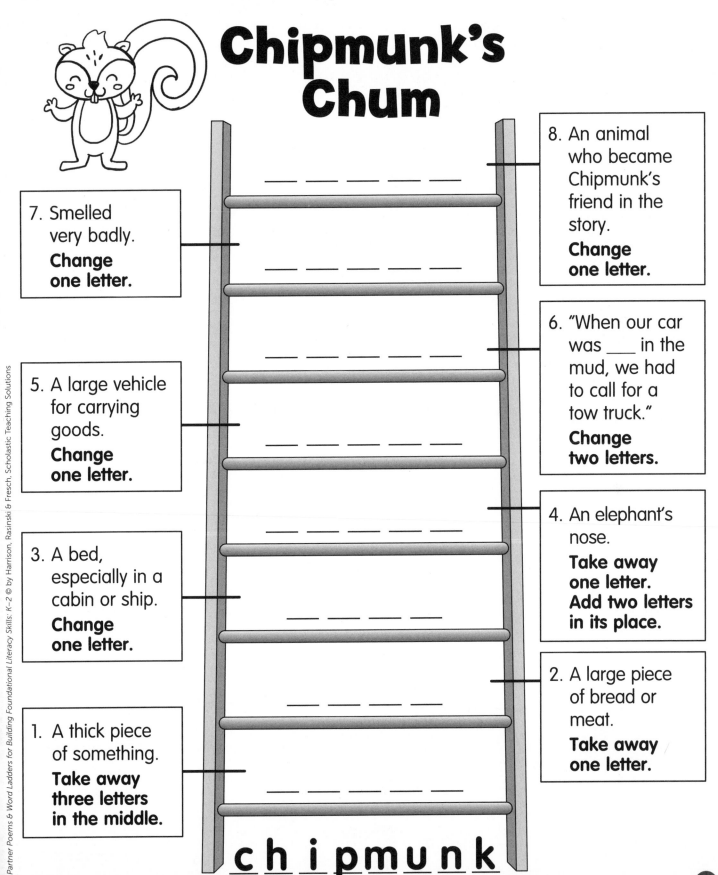

Chipmunk's Chum

8. An animal who became Chipmunk's friend in the story. **Change one letter.**

7. Smelled very badly. **Change one letter.**

6. "When our car was ___ in the mud, we had to call for a tow truck." **Change two letters.**

5. A large vehicle for carrying goods. **Change one letter.**

4. An elephant's nose. **Take away one letter. Add two letters in its place.**

3. A bed, especially in a cabin or ship. **Change one letter.**

2. A large piece of bread or meat. **Take away one letter.**

1. A thick piece of something. **Take away three letters in the middle.**

c h i p m u n k

Partner Poems & Word Ladders for Building Foundational Literacy Skills: K–2 © by Harrison, Rasinski & Fresch, Scholastic Teaching Solutions

117

Tic-Tac-Toe

Objective: Children will read -*unk* words to play a game.

Materials

- "Deep in the Woods" (page 114)
- chart paper or whiteboard
- 9 index cards (for each pair of children)
- tic-tac-toe grid drawn on paper (see right)
- pencils
- game markers of two different colors or shapes (e.g., two colors of buttons)

Tic-Tac-Toe

(Available online.)

Procedure

1. Invite children to read the poem several times, letting different pairs of children take turns reading 1st Voice and 2nd Voice while the rest of the class reads the All Together voice.

2. Have children find the -*unk* words in the poem. Ask if they know any others and make a list on the board or chart paper.

3. Pair up children. Then pass out the tic-tac-toe grid and index cards to each pair.

4. Read aloud nine -*unk* words from the poem and suggested list, one at a time. Have one partner write each word in the grid wherever he or she chooses, while the other partner writes each word on an index card.

5. Have partners choose their game markers (color/shape). Have them turn the index cards facedown and shuffle them around.

-*unk* words		
bunk	chunk	**chipmunk**
dunk	clunk	chunky
funk	drunk	clunker
gunk	flunk	funky
hunk	**plunk**	junkyard
junk	shrunk	preshrunk
punk	**skunk**	shrunken
sunk	slunk	spelunking
	stunk	spunky
	trunk	

6. To play, one child picks a facedown card and reads aloud the word on it. The child uses his or her marker to cover that word on the tic-tac-toe grid. Partners continue taking turns picking a card, reading the word, and then covering it on the tic-tac-toe grid. Game ends when someone gets tic-tac-toe or when all the cards are used up. (This is an easy game to add to a workstation for the children to revisit later in the day.)

Assessment: Do the children correctly spell and read aloud the -*unk* words? Listen in as they play the game to see who might need further support and review.

Shoo, Fly!

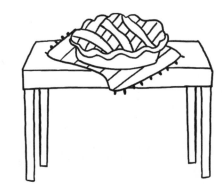

1st Voice

Hi.

I'm a little fly.

I loved your pie.

Oh, my.
You mustn't cry.
I only ate
a little pie.
Dry your eye.

By the way,
I loved your ham.

With a bite of yam
and yummy jam.

Off I go,
flying high,
but I'll be back
for a little more pie.

2nd Voice

Who are you?

Well, little fly,
just fly on by.

No! No!
Not my pie!
Don't want a fly
eating my pie!

Sigh.
I'll try.

You ate my ham?

That's it.
Scram!

Read the clues. Then, write the words.
Start at the bottom and climb to the top.

Just Dessert

7. A dessert that
the fly in the
poem ate.
**Change
one letter.**

___ ___ ___ ___

6. A hole in
the ground.
**Move the
letters around.**

5. The pointed
end of
something.
**Change
one letter.**

___ ___ ___

4. To tear
something.
**Take away
one letter.**

___ ___ ___ ___

3. To stumble
or fall. Also,
a journey.
**Take away
one letter.
Add two
letters in
its place.**

___ ___ ___ ___

2. To attempt to
do something.
**Change
one letter.**

___ ___ ___ ___

1. To cook food
in hot oil.
**Change
one letter.**

___ ___ ___

f l y

Name _____

Read the clues. Then, write the words.
Start at the bottom and climb to the top.

Fly By

8. A yellow fat used for cooking. Also, combined with the first word, an insect with broad, beautiful wings.
Change one letter.

7. In baseball, the player who tries to hit the ball.
Add three letters to the end.

6. A flying mammal. Also, an item used to hit a baseball.
Change one letter.

5. An animal like a mouse, only bigger.
Change one letter.

4. A male sheep.
Take away one letter.

3. To stuff things into a small space.
Take away one letter. Add two letters in its place.

2. To shed tears.
Change one letter.

1. To cook food in hot oil or fat.
Change one letter.

f l y

Partner Poems & Word Ladders for Building Foundational Literacy Skills: K–2 © by Harrison, Rasinski & Fresch, Scholastic Teaching Solutions

I Spy

Objective: Children will identify -y words.

Materials

- "Shoo, Fly!" (page 119)
- chart paper or whiteboard

Procedure

1. Invite children to read the poem several times, letting different pairs of children take turns to read 1st Voice and 2nd Voice.

2. Ask children what they notice about the words that rhyme. *(long-i sound spelled with y)*

3. On chart paper or the board, make a list of the -y words from the poem. (You might discuss the words *hi, pie, eye, sigh,* and *high,* which have the long-*i* sound but are spelled differently.) Ask children if they know any other -y words and add these to the list. You might prompt by asking them to think about consonant blends, such as *fr, pl, sp,* and so on.

-y words		
by	**cry**	butterfly
my	**dry**	deny
	fly	firefly
	fry	July
	ply	lullaby
	pry	
	shy	
	sky	
	sly	
	spry	
	spy	
	try	
	why	

4. Play the "I Spy" game, telling children you will give a clue to one of the words written on the list. Begin by saying, "I spy with my little eye a word that begins with m." Call on a volunteer to read that word. *(my)* Play continues with that child saying, "I spy with my little eye a word that begins with . . ." Continue until all children have had a turn. For more challenge, use definitions as clues (e.g., "I spy with my little eye a month of the year.").

Assessment: Are children able to suggest any words? Could they read the chosen word aloud?

Wondering about eye?

Eye comes from an Old English word *ege* meaning "the eye region." The sound that is represented as *g* does not exist in modern English, and over time the sound became represented as *y*.

References

Bridgeland, J., & Bruce, M. (2013). *The missing piece: A national teacher survey on how social and emotional learning can empower children and transform schools*. Collaborative for Academic, Social, and Emotional Learning.

Fresch, M. J. (2019). Poetry across the curriculum: An approach for learning vocabulary and content. *Missouri Reader, 42*(2), 14–17.

Fry, E. (1998). The most common phonograms. *The Reading Teacher, 51*, 620–622.

Gill, S. R. (2007). The forgotten genre of children's poetry. *The Reading Teacher, 60*, 622–625.

Menon, S., & Hiebert, E. H. (2005). A comparison of first graders' reading with little books or literature-based basal anthologies. *Reading Research Quarterly, 40*(1), 12–38.

Online Etymology Dictionary. https://www.etymoline.com.

Perfect, K. A. (1999). Rhyme and reason: Poetry for the heart and head. *The Reading Teacher, 52*, 728–737.

Pierce, L. (2011). *Repeated readings in poetry versus prose: Fluency and enjoyment for second graders*. [Unpublished doctoral dissertation]. University of Toledo.

Rasinski, T. (2008). *Daily word ladders: Grades 1–2*. Scholastic.

Rasinski, T. (2012). *Daily word ladders: Grades K–1*. Scholastic.

Rasinski, T. (2020, September 12). Why poetry? Let me count the ways. *The Robb Review*. https://therobbreviewblog.com/uncategorized/poetry/.

Rasinski, T., Harrison, D. L., & Fawcett, G. (2009). *Partner poems for building fluency*. Scholastic.

Rasinski, T., Rupley, W. H., & Nichols, W. D. (2012). *Phonics and fluency practice with poetry*. Scholastic.

Rasinski, T., & Stevenson, B. (2005). The effects of fast start reading, a fluency-based home involvement reading program, on the reading achievement of beginning readers. *Reading Psychology: An International Quarterly, 26*, 109–125.

Rasinski, T. V., & Zimmerman, B. (2013). What's the perfect text for struggling readers? Try poetry! *Reading Today, 30*, 15–16.

Rasinski, T. V., & Zimmerman, B. (2015, July). Guest-edited issue of the *New England Reading Association Journal* devoted to poetry.

Seitz, S. (2013). Poetic fluency. *The Reading Teacher, 67*, 312–314.

Shanahan, T. (2016, June 26). Further explanation of teaching students with challenging text. *Shanahan on Literacy*. Accessed at https://shanahanonliteracy.com/blog/further-explanation-of-teaching-students-with-challenging-text.

Stahl, S., & Heubach, K. (2005). Fluency-oriented reading instruction. *Journal of Literacy Research, 37*, 25–60.

Wilfong, L. G. (2008). Building fluency, word-recognition ability, and confidence in struggling readers: The poetry academy. *The Reading Teacher, 62*(1), 4–13.

Wylie, R. E., & Durrell, D. D. (1970). Teaching vowels through phonograms. *Elementary School Journal, 47*, 787–791.

Word Ladder Template

Read the clues. Then, write the words.
Start at the bottom and climb to the top.

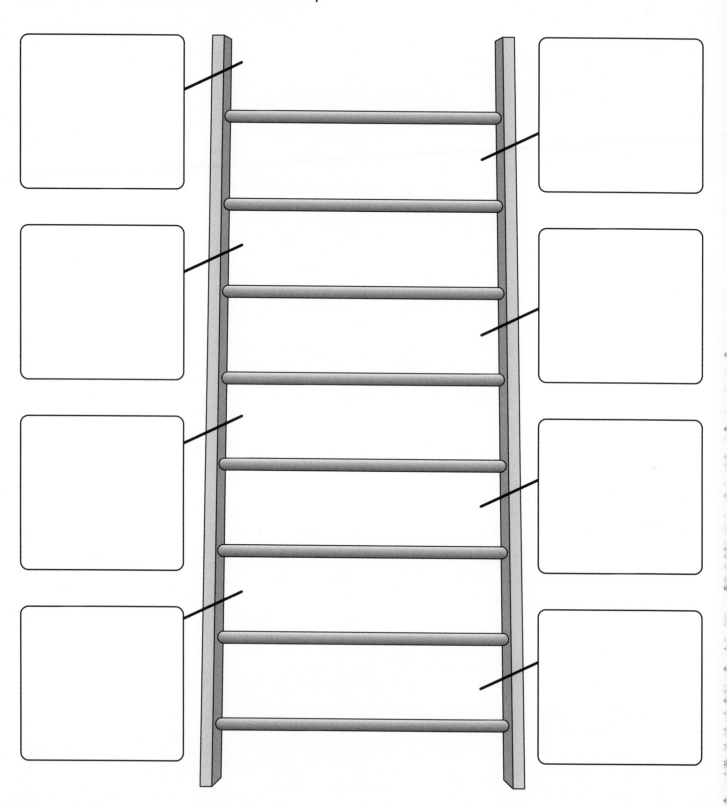

Consonant Letter Cards

b	c	d	f	g
h	j	k	l	m
n	p	r	s	t
v	w	x	y	z
qu				

Partner Poems & Word Ladders for Building Foundational Literacy Skills: K–2 © by Harrison, Rasinski & Fresch, Scholastic Teaching Solutions

Consonant Cluster Cards

bl	br	cl
cr	dr	fl
fr	gl	gr
pl	pr	sc
sk	sl	sm

sn	sp	spl
spr	st	str
sw	tr	tw
ch	ph	sh
th	wh	

Answer Key (Word Ladders)

-ab
page 13: 1. grab 2. crab 3. cab 4. jab 5. job 6. lob 7. lab 8. blab
page 14: 1. mister 2. mist 3. mast 4. last 5. lay 6. lab 7. crab 8. crabby

-ack
page 17: 1. buck 2. back 3. tack 4. tuck 5. cluck 6. click 7. quick 8. quack
page 18: 1. tack 2. tackle 3. tickle 4. pickle 5. pick 6. pack 7. yack 8. yak

-ag
page 21: 1. big 2. wig 3. wag 4. rag 5. tag 6. sag 7. nag
page 22: 1. stuck 2. tuck 3. tug 4. tag 5. stag 6. brag 7. bag

-am
page 25: 1. men 2. man 3. ran 4. ram 5. scram 6. cram 7. jam 8. Pam
page 26: 1. crack 2. cram 3. scram 4. scramble 5. ram 6. Sam 7. slam 8. jam

-an
page 29: 1. man 2. fan 3. ran 4. rag 5. bag 6. tag 7. tan
page 30: 1. six 2. sip 3. slip 4. clip 5. clap 6. clan 7. fan

-ank
page 33: 1. tea 2. ten 3. tan 4. tank 5. clank 6. blank 7. bank 8. rank
page 34: 1. prank 2. rank 3. bank 4. tank 5. talk 6. stalk 7. walk

-ap
page 38: 1. sap 2. lap 3. flap 4. clap 5. chap 6. chat 7. hat
page 39: 1. in 2. pin 3. pan 4. nap 5. clap 6. clamp 7. champ 8. chap

-at
page 42: 1. chat 2. cat 3. bat 4. bit 5. pit 6. pet 7. pat 8. hat
page 43: 1. cattle 2. rattle 3. rat 4. bat 5. bag 6. big 7. dig 8. dog

-ay
page 47: 1. clay 2. play 3. pay 4. gay 5. gab 6. grab 7. gray
page 48: 1. monkey 2. money 3. on 4. ton 5. toy 6. boy 7. bay 8. bray

-ed
page 51: 1. red 2. sled 3. slid 4. lid 5. bid 6. bad 7. bed 8. Ted
page 52: 1. clover 2. cover 3. cove 4. move 5. me 6. we 7. wed 8. red

-ill
page 55: 1. ball 2. mall 3. small 4. stall 5. still 6. spill 7. pill 8. Jill
page 56: 1. wind 2. wand 3. want 4. pant 5. pint 6. pit 7. pill 8. hill

-im
page 60: 1. slim 2. slip 3. lip 4. tip 5. trip 6. trim 7. grim
page 61: 1. food 2. brood 3. broom 4. brim 5. rim 6. rid 7. bid 8. bad

-in
page 64: 1. win 2. fin 3. fan 4. fall 5. fill 6. gill 7. Jill
page 65: 1. spin 2. shin 3. skin 4. skim 5. skill 6. still 7. stink 8. tin

-ing
page 69: 1. ring 2. wing 3. swing 4. sing 5. sting 6. string 7. spring
page 70: 1. end 2. den 3. pen 4. pin 5. win 6. swing 7. sling 8. sing

-ink
page 74: 1. blank 2. bank 3. tank 4. thank 5. think 6. pink 7. wink
page 75: 1. rink 2. shrink 3. stink 4. sting 5. sing 6. sink 7. mink 8. milk

-ip
page 79: 1. flip 2. flap 3. lap 4. clap 5. clip 6. slip 7. ship 8. hip
page 80: 1. zap 2. map 3. mop 4. top 5. tap 6. trap 7. trip 8. tip

-it
page 83: 1. skit 2. spit 3. split 4. pit 5. pat 6. hat 7. hit
page 84: 1. hard 2. card 3. car 4. scar 5. scat 6. skit 7. sit 8. fit

-ob
page 87: 1. job 2. jab 3. cab 4. cob 5. sob 6. lob 7. Bob
page 88: 1. frown 2. brown 3. brow 4. bow 5. bob 6. rob 7. rose 8. nose

-op
page 91: 1. pain 2. pin 3. nip 4. nap 5. tap 6. top 7. stop 8. drop
page 92: 1. pin 2. tin 3. ton 4. top 5. hop 6. hon 7. hen 8. pen

-ot
page 95: 1. cot 2. hot 3. shot 4. shop 5. chop 6. cop 7. top 8. tot
page 96: 1. shop 2. stop 3. spot 4. post 5. pot 6. potter 7. hotter

-uck
page 99: 1. cluck 2. luck 3. lick 4. sick 5. sack 6. tack 7. track 8. truck
page 100: 1. stuck 2. duck 3. dock 4. do 5. go 6. gold 7. good 8. wood

-ug
page 103: 1. tug 2. tag 3. rag 4. rug 5. hug 6. chug 7. jug
page 104: 1. lug 2. log 3. lot 4. trot 5. rot 6. rut 7. cut 8. cup

-um
page 107: 1. hum 2. hut 3. hot 4. hop 5. mop 6. mom 7. mum
page 108: 1. bother 2. both 3. bot 4. rot 5. rut 6. strut 7. strum 8. drum

-ump
page 111: 1. hump 2. ump 3. lump 4. clump 5. cluck 6. clack 7. crack
page 112: 1. clump 2. clamp 3. lamp 4. lack 5. back 6. buck 7. bump 8. stump

-unk
page 116: 1. gunk 2. dunk 3. duck 4. tuck 5. tick 6. trick 7. trunk
page 117: 1. chunk 2. hunk 3. bunk 4. trunk 5. truck 6. stuck 7. stunk 8. skunk

-y
page 120: 1. fry 2. try 3. trip 4. rip 5. tip 6. pit 7. pie
page 121: 1. fry 2. cry 3. cram 4. ram 5. rat 6. bat 7. batter 8. butter